唱新歌 | 学汉语

SING SONGS AND

对 外 汉 语 选 修 课 教 材　　王晓音 / 编著

LEARN CHINESE

北京语言大学出版社
BEIJING LANGUAGE AND CULTURE
UNIVERSITY PRESS

（京）新登字 157 号

图书在版编目（CIP）数据

唱新歌 学汉语 / 王晓音编著 . —北京：北京语言大
学出版社，2007.8
ISBN 978-7-5619-1923-1

Ⅰ.唱… Ⅱ.王… Ⅲ.①汉语-对外汉语教学-语言读物
②创作歌曲-作品集-中国-现代 Ⅳ.H195.5：J

中国版本图书馆 CIP 数据核字（2007）第 124793 号

书　　　名：唱新歌 学汉语
中文编辑：王　轩　　英文编辑：鲁　霞
封面设计：周文辉
责任印制：汪学发

出版发行：北京语言大学出版社
社　　址：北京市海淀区学院路 15 号　邮政编码：100083
网　　址：www.blcup.com
电　　话：发行部　82303650/3591/3651
　　　　　编辑部　82303647
　　　　　读者服务部　82303653/3908
印　　刷：北京中科印刷有限公司
经　　销：全国新华书店

版　　次：2007 年 8 月第 1 版　2007 年 8 月第 1 次印刷
开　　本：787 毫米×1000 毫米　1/16　印张：14.5
字　　数：177 千字　　　印数：1 - 3000
书　　号：ISBN 978-7-5619-1923-1/H·07144
定　　价：33.00 元

凡有印装质量问题，本社负责调换。电话：82303590

使·用·说·明

　　《唱新歌 学汉语》是为外国留学生编选的学唱中国歌曲的教材，可供具有初级汉语水平的外国留学生汉语节目表演用。

　　本书选取中国当代歌曲，以二十世纪八九十年代及二十一世纪流行歌曲为主，选取原则有以下几点：流行时间长、范围广；曲调、旋律流畅，易学唱；歌词易学易记，适合作为外国留学生学习汉语的辅助材料。

　　全书共三部分，十八首歌曲。按照时代划分为"八十年代老歌""九十年代好歌""新世纪新歌"三辑。每一辑有"时代背景"介绍相关时代背景知识；每辑六首歌，每首由"学唱""歌词""歌中词语""歌中句式""歌手""作者"等板块组成，包含了曲谱、歌词、生词、语法、歌曲背景知识等内容。

　　本书的编写得到了董璐、王乐、徐亮、欧阳文思、李敏的帮助，在此表示感谢。

陕西师范大学国际汉学院

王晓音

Instructions

Sing Songs and Learn Chinese is compiled for international students who are beginners of Chinese to learn Chinese pop songs.

The book selects modern Chinese songs, mainly the popular songs of the 1980s to the 21st century. Characterized by lasting popularity and beautiful melody, these songs are suitable and are easy to learn for international students to learn Chinese as a supplementary learning material.

The book contains 18 songs in three parts: "Old Favorites in the 80's", "Pop Songs in the 90's", and "New Song in the New Century". There are 6 songs and background information in each part. Each lesson includes the following sections, Sing Together, Lyrics, Vocabulary, Grammar Notes, About the Singer, About the Writer, etc., providing the music score, lyrics, vocabulary, grammar and related information.

Many people contributed to the compilation of this book. Special thanks go to Ms. Dong Lu, Ms. Wang Le, Mr. Xu Liang, Ms. Ouyang Wensi and Ms. Li Min.

Wang Xiaoyin
The International College of Chinese Studies
Shaanxi Normal University

Contents 目录

唱新歌｜学汉语

SING SONGS AND LEARN CHINESE

Old Favorites in the 80's
八十年代老歌

一 《思念》Sīniàn

学唱 → Sing Together

毛阿敏　演唱
乔羽　　词
谷建芬　　曲

你从哪里来？　　我的朋友，

好像一只蝴蝶　飞进我的窗口。

不知能作　　几日停留，

我们已经分　别得太久太　久。

你从哪里来？　　我的朋友，你

好像一只蝴蝶飞进我的窗　　口。

为何 你一去 便无 消息?

只把思念 积 压在我心 头。
D.C.

难道 你又要 匆匆 离去?

又把聚会 当 成一次分 手。
Fine.

Nǐ cóng nǎli lái? Wǒ de péngyou,
你 从 哪里来? 我 的 朋友,

hǎoxiàng yì zhī húdié fēijìn wǒ de chuāngkǒu.
好像 一只 蝴蝶 飞进 我 的 窗口。

Bù zhī néng zuò jǐ rì tíngliú,
不 知 能 作 几日 停留,

wǒmen yǐjīng fēnbié de tài jiǔ tài jiǔ.
我们 已经 分别 得 太久太久。

Nǐ cóng nǎli lái? Wǒ de péngyou,
你 从 哪里来? 我 的 朋友,

nǐ hǎoxiàng yì zhī húdié fēijìn wǒ de chuāngkǒu.
你 好像 一只 蝴蝶 飞进 我 的 窗口。

Wèihé nǐ yí qù biàn wú xiāoxi?

为何 你 一 去 便 无 消息？

Zhǐ bǎ sīniàn jīyā zài wǒ xīntóu.

只 把 思念 积压 在 我 心头。

Nándào nǐ yòu yào cōngcōng líqù?

难道 你 又 要 匆匆 离去？

Yòu bǎ jùhuì dāngchéng yí cì fēnshǒu.

又 把 聚会 当成 一 次 分手。

　　这首歌描写的是老朋友分别很久后短暂相聚，不忍离别的心情。

　　朋友不期而至，就像一只蝴蝶飞进窗口那样意外。这次到来，能不能多待些日子？我们分别太久了，有好多话要说呢。不要走得那么匆忙，像上次一样，一走就再也没有了音信，让我苦苦地思念这么久。"相见时难别亦难"，虽然所有的相聚都会以分手告终，但我真的不希望这么快就说再见。

This song describes the sentimental feelings that old friends feel when they meet after being separated for a long time.

　　My dear friend, here you come, just like a butterfly flying into the window. Could you stay longer this time? We've parted for such a long time, and I've got a lot to talk to you. Please don't leave me in such a hurry! After you left the last time, I haven't heard from you for so long and have been missing you so much. As a famous poem reads, "Hard it was to see each other, hard still to part." Although all feasts must come to an end, I don't want to say goodbye to you so soon.

▶▶ 歌中词语 Vocabuary

1. 思念	sīniàn	to miss
2. 能	néng	(expressing possibility) can
3. 停留	tíngliú	to stay
4. 分别	fēnbié	to leave each other, to part
5. 为何	wèihé	why
6. 消息	xiāoxi	news, message
7. 积压	jīyā	to accumulate, to overstock
8. 难道	nándào	could it be that
9. 匆匆	cōngcōng	hurriedly
10. 聚会	jùhuì	to meet, to get together
11. 分手	fēn shǒu	to say goodbye, to part

▶▶ 歌中句式 Grammer Notes

1. 作几日停留

"作"，指从事某种活动。

"作" means to do, to make.

例如：稍作休息

不作解释

2. 一去便无消息

"去"，离开。"便"，就。一离开就没有了音信。

"去"means to leave. "便" means "as soon as". The sentence means that nothing is heard from the friend ever since he/she leaves.

"一……就……"表示两件事紧接着发生。

"一……就……" means that one thing happens very quickly right after another.

例如：我一下课就去。

他一回来，我就告诉你。

3. 把思念积压在我心头

"把"字句，表示对事物的处置。"把"后面的动词要带其他成分，"把+名+动+介词短语"是常见格式之一。

The "把" sentence is used to indicate the result of an action or the influence an action has on something or somebody. The verb after "把" usually takes other components. The common structure is "把+Noun+Verb+Propositional Phrase".

例如：老师把书放在桌子上。

请你把这封信带给小王。

4. 把聚会当成一次分手

"把……当成……"表示如何看待某人或某事。"当成" 可换用为 "当做"。

"把……当成……" means "take... as ...". "当成" can also be replaced by "当做".

例如：我把他当成最好的朋友。
我把盐当做糖了。

5. 难道你又要匆匆离去

"又"表示前一动作或情况重复出现。

"又" indicates that the preceding action or state of affairs appears again.

例如：昨天他来过，今天又来了。
你刚吃完饭，怎么又饿了？

毛阿敏（Mao Amin）

1963 年 3 月生于上海。做了两年纺织工人后，参军入伍，先后到南京军区前线歌舞团、总政歌舞团当独唱演员。曾在著名作曲家谷建芬的声乐培训中心接受专业训练，1986 年在全国青年歌手电视大奖赛中获"通俗唱法"第三名。

1987 年 12 月，南斯拉夫第四届"贝尔格莱德国际音乐节"上，毛阿敏以《绿叶对根的情意》获奖，成为第一位在国际流行音乐赛事上获奖的中国内地歌手。评委们评价她的演唱"入情忘我，具有东方女性温柔典雅的魅力"。她的获奖，使中国内地流行音乐开始走向世界。

毛阿敏的声音宽厚高亢、深沉沧桑，演唱风格雍容大方、端庄稳重，情绪表达真切自然、感人肺腑。1988 年中国中央电视台春节联欢晚会上，毛阿敏演唱《思念》，一举成名，之后的电视剧《渴望》主题歌是她艺术生涯的高峰。为许多电视剧、大型晚会演唱，使毛阿敏确定了内地"顶尖实力派歌星"的地位。

代表作：《思念》《绿叶对根的情意》《渴望》《同一首歌》等。

Mao Amin was born in Shanghai in March, 1963. She worked as a textile worker for two years and then was enlisted in the army as a vocalist in Nan Jing Front Song-and-Dance Ensemble of the General Political Department of the Chinese PLA. She received professional training in the vocal training center founded by the famous composer Gu Jianfen. In 1986, she won the third prize as a pop-song singer in the CCTV National Young Singers' Contest.

In December, 1987, Mao won an award in the fourth International Music Festival in Belgrade, Yugoslavia with the song "The Affection of Leaves towards the Root", which made her the first singer from mainland China to receive an award in an international popular music competition. Her performance was commented as "passionate with tenderness and elegancy of an oriental lady". Her winning the prize was the first step for the popular music of China's mainland to go out to the world.

Thanks to her resounding and resonant voice, decent and elegant performance and natural and touching expression of feelings, Mao became famous overnight by singing the song "Missing" in the CCTV Spring Festival Gala in 1988. Later the singing of the theme song of the TV serial "Longing" marked the peak of her career. Her excellent performance on stage and for TV serials made her one of the top pop singers in mainland China.

Representative Songs: "Missing", "The Affection of Leaves towards the Root", "Longing", "The Same Song".

《思念》的词作者乔羽，1927年出生，山东人。从20世纪50年代年代至今，创作了《我的祖国》《让我们荡起双桨》《难忘今宵》《爱我中华》等经典歌曲，是新中国歌词创作高峰的代表，被评价为"词坛泰斗"。运用平实质朴的语言、智慧幽默的手法，表达美好善良的感情，是乔羽的创作特色。

许多人都问乔羽，《思念》中的这只"蝴蝶"，是代表友情还是爱情？其实这里有一个小故事。1963年夏天的一个下午，乔羽回到家，打开窗户，忽然飞进来一只金黄色的蝴蝶，它自由自在地在屋子里飞了好几圈。乔羽有些吃惊，但没有惊动它，看着它又从窗口飞了出去。那一刻，他的心中涌起一种说不出的感动。1988年，他在创作一首咏叹友谊的歌曲时，开启了25前的那段回忆，写下了《思念》这首经久不衰的好歌。这是他一千多首歌词中创作时间最长的一首。

The lyricist of this song, Qiao Yu, was born in 1927 in Shandong Province. As one of the leading lyricists in China from 1950s till now, Qiao has produced a lot of classics, such as "My Fatherland", "Let's Row the Boat", "Tonight is unforgettable" and "Ode to China", which are all representative of the best of New China's lyrical works. Qiao is regarded as the lord of the lyric world in new China. His works are characterized by simple and plain language with a sense of humor to express the beauty and kindness of human nature.

People often ask Qiao Yu what "the butterfly" in the song "Missing" represents, friendship or love? Here is the story. One summer day in 1963 when Qiao came back home, on opening the window, a golden butterfly flied into his room and circled freely for several minutes. Qiao was very surprised and watched it quietly until it flied out when he felt a sudden unspeakable touch of his heart. Twenty five years later in 1988, this scene jumped into his mind when he was writing a song on friendship, which is the famous song "Missing".

二《一无所有》

Yī Wú Suǒ Yǒu

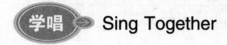 学唱 → Sing Together

崔　健　演唱
崔　健　词曲

1. 我 曾 经 问 个 不 休，　　　你 何 时 跟 我 走?
2. 脚 下 这 地 在 走，　　　身 边 那 水 在 流。
3. 告诉你 我 等 了 很 久，　　告诉你 我 最后的 要 求，

可 你 却 总 是 笑　　我，一 无 所 有。
可 你 却 总 是 笑　　我，一 无 所 有。
我 要 抓 起 你 的 双　　手，你 这就 跟 我 走。

‖¹ 1. 我 要 给 你 我 的 追　　求，　　　还 有 我 的 自

¹²³ 2. 为 何 你 总 笑 个 没　　够?　　　为 何 我 总 要　　追
3. 这 时 你 的 手 在 颤　　抖，　　　这 时 你 的 泪 在

由，　　　可 你 却 总 是 笑　　我，

求?　　　难 道 在 你 面 前 我　永　　远是
流，　　　莫 非 你 是 正 在　告诉　　我，

一 无 所 有。　　1/2. 噢……　　　你
　　　　　　　　3. 噢……　　　你
你爱我 一无 所 有。

何 时 跟 我 走?　　1/2. 噢……　　　你
这 就 跟 我 走。　　3. 噢……　　　你

D.C.

何 时 跟 我 　走?
这 就 跟 我 　走。

歌词　Lyrics

Wǒ céngjīng wèn ge bù xiū, nǐ héshí gēn wǒ zǒu?
我　曾经　问 个不休,你何时　跟 我 走?

kě nǐ què zǒngshì xiào wǒ, yī wú suǒ yǒu.
可你却　总是 笑 我,一无 所 有。

Wǒ yào gěi nǐ wǒ de zhuīqiú, hái yǒu wǒ de zìyóu,
我 要 给你我 的 追求, 还 有 我 的 自由,

kě nǐ què zǒngshì xiào wǒ, yī wú suǒ yǒu.
可你却 总是 笑 我,一无 所 有。

Ō …… Nǐ héshí gēn wǒ zǒu?
噢…… 你 何时 跟 我 走?

Jiǎoxià zhè dì zài zǒu, shēnbiān nà shuǐ zài liú,
脚下　这 地在 走, 身边 那 水 在流,

kě nǐ què zǒngshì xiào wǒ, yī wú suǒ yǒu.

可你却 总是 笑 我，一无 所 有。

Wèihé nǐ zǒng xiào ge méi gòu?

为何 你总 笑 个 没 够？

Wèihé wǒ zǒng yào zhuīqiú?

为何 我 总 要 追求？

Nándào zài nǐ miànqián wǒ yǒngyuǎn shì yī wú suǒ yǒu.

难道 在你 面前 我 永远 是一无 所 有。

Ō…… Nǐ héshí gēn wǒ zǒu?

噢…… 你 何时 跟 我 走？

Gàosu nǐ wǒ děngle hěn jiǔ,

告诉 你我 等了 很 久，

gàosu nǐ wǒ zuìhòu de yāoqiú,

告诉 你我 最后 的 要求，

wǒ yào zhuāqǐ nǐ de shuāngshǒu,

我 要 抓起 你的 双手，

nǐ zhè jiù gēn wǒ zǒu.

你 这就 跟 我 走。

Zhè shí nǐ de shǒu zài chàndǒu, zhè shí nǐ de lèi zài liú,

这 时你的 手 在 颤抖， 这 时你的 泪在 流，

mòfēi nǐ shì zhèngzài gàosu wǒ,

莫非 你是 正在 告诉 我，

nǐ ài wǒ yī wú suǒyǒu.

你爱我 一无 所有。

Ō…… Nǐ zhè jiù gēn wǒ zǒu.

噢…… 你 这就 跟 我 走。

●●● 歌词大意 Main Idea of the Lyrics ●●●

　　这首歌是一个大胆的爱情宣言。

　　"我一无所有，可是我爱你，你什么时候跟我走呢？"
"一无所有？拿什么来承担爱情的责任呢？""一个自由
的生命及其所追求的梦想，不比任何物质更宝贵吗？"一
颗执著的心，等待良久，终于打动了芳心；颤抖的手、
流淌的泪，这正是无言的回答：如果你值得我爱，哪怕
你一无所有！

　　It is a daring love statement.

　　"I've got nothing to my name. But I love you so
much. When will you go with me?" "Nothing to your
name? How can you take on the responsibility for
love?" "A free soul with all his dreams is more precious
than anything else, isn't it?" The persistent heart, after
waiting for so long, finally touched the girl. Hands trem-
bling, tears dripping, she answered in silence: you are
worth loving even though you have nothing to your
name!

▶▶ 歌中词语　Vocabuary

1. 一无所有	yī wú suǒ yǒu	to have nothing
2. 曾经	céngjīng	once, ever
3. 休	xiū	to stop
4. 何时	héshí	when
5. 总是	zǒngshì	always
6. 追求	zhuīqiú	to pursue
7. 自由	zìyóu	freedom
8. 流	liú	to flow
9. 永远	yǒngyuǎn	forever
10. 久	jiǔ	(long) time
11. 最后	zuìhòu	at last, finally
12. 要求	yāoqiú	demand
13. 抓	zhuā	to grab
14. 颤抖	chàndǒu	to quiver, to tremble
15. 莫非	mòfēi	can it be possible that

▶▶ 歌中句式　Grammer Notes

1. 问个不休／笑个没够

　　"动+个+形／动" 用法中，"个" 的作用是引进动词的

补语。动词可带"了"。否定式是"动+个+不／没+形/动"。

In this structure "Verb+个+Adj.／Verb","个"introduces the complement of the verb."了"can be added after the verb. The negative form is "V+个+不／没+A/V".

例如：看个仔细
说个不停

2. 总是笑我

"笑"，在这里是"嘲笑"的意思。

"笑" here means "to laugh at".

例如：同学不会回答问题时，大家不要笑他。
你别笑奶奶不会上网，她年纪大了。

3. 地在走／水在流

"在"，在这里是副词，意思是"正在"。

"在" is an adverb here, meaning "in the process of".

例如：我们在上自习。
这条路在修，不能走。

4. 抓起你的双手

"动+起+名"用法中，"起"是趋向动词，表示动作的向上方向。

In the structure "Verb + 起 + Noun", "起" is a directional verb indicating the upward direction of the action.

例如：他拿起雨伞就出门了。

老李抬起头看了看。

5．这就跟你走

"就+动/形"用法中，"就"是副词，表示事情或动作很快将要发生。可与"这"连用，"这"表示说话的同时。

In the structure "就 + Verb / Adj.", "就" is an adverb indicating that the action will happen soon. "这" can be used at the beginning of the sentence to emphasize the immediate happening of action following the utterance.

例如：别着急，我这就去。

我明天就回去。

歌手
About the Singer

崔健（Cui Jian）

　　1961 年 8 月崔健出生于一个朝鲜族家庭。父亲是专业的小号演奏者，母亲是朝鲜族舞蹈团的成员。1981 年，崔健成为北京交响乐团的小号演奏员。80 年代中期，西方摇滚音乐的影响使他开始了自己的摇滚乐创作，1984 年成立"七合板乐队"。

　　1986 年，纪念国际和平年百名歌星演唱会上，崔健穿了一件像是清朝服装的长褂子，背着一把破吉他，两只裤脚一高一低，蹦上舞台，观众不明白发生了什么。音乐响起，崔健吼出"我曾经问个不休，你何时跟我走……"，台下变得静悄悄的。歌曲结束，被震撼的观众热烈欢呼、起立鼓掌。中国内地的摇滚乐诞生了，第一位摇滚歌星诞生了。

　　从那时到现在，崔健一直作为中国摇滚乐的领军人物活跃在歌坛，影响力很大，被称为"中国摇滚的奠基者""中国摇滚教父"。2006 年 7 月，他获得了华语音乐传媒大奖"殿堂音乐家奖"。

　　代表作：《一无所有》《新长征路上的摇滚》《花房姑娘》《快让我在雪地上撒点儿野》等。

Cui Jian was born in a Korean ethnic family in August 1961. His father is a professional trumpet player and his mother a member of a Korean minority dance troupe. In 1981 Cui Jian became a trumpet player with the prestigious Beijing Phiharmonic Orchestra. In mid 80s, he began creating rock music under the influence of the Western rock and roll, and in 1984 he and six other musicians formed the Seven-Ply-Board Band.

In 1986, at a Beijing concert commemorating the Year of the World Peace, Cui Jian jamped onto the stage in a long garment of Qing-Dynasty style. With a worn guitar, he belted out "I kept asking you when you can go with me", and the spectators were all in silence. When the song ended, the stunned audience erupted in a standing ovation. The rock and roll of mainland China was born! We had our first rock star! From that time on, Cui has been active in musical circle as a leader of Chinese rock music and has been very influential. He is regarded as "the founder of Chinese rock music" and "father of Chinese rock'n'roll". He won the Hall Musician Award of the Chinese Music Media Awards in July 2006.

Representative Songs: "Nothing to My Name", "Rock and Roll on the New Long March", "The Girl in the Flower Shop", "Let Me Act Wildly on Snowy Earth Immediately".

当时，进行曲、抒情歌曲和流行歌曲，都是"别人"的歌，平凡的人们渴望发出自己的声音。这时，崔健和《一无所有》出现了。他在歌词中第一次用第一人称"我"来表达爱情，真实而大胆地表达自我意识，人们觉得，崔健毫不修饰的呐喊的歌声就是自己的，他唱的就是自己的感觉。

直白的语言加上狂放的旋律，这首歌让人们的精神找到了一个出口。演唱会上姑娘们流着泪喊"崔健，我跟你走！"的场景，永远留在了那一代人的记忆里。崔健说自己写的只是一个情歌，并没有很多的期待；然而，这首歌被时代赋予了超越本身的意义，已经成为一个历史的符号、一个年代的印记。

During that special period of time, ordinary people longed for shouting out their own voices instead of singing marches, pop songs and lyric songs which are "others' songs". By his "Nothing to My Name", Cui Jian was the first one to use "I" to boldly express love and self-awareness. It's considered that his unembellished shouting is the expression of his true feelings.

In straightforward language and unruly melody, this song finally offered a chance for people to release their feelings. The scene of girls screaming in tears "Cui Jian! I wanna go with you!" at the concert will remain in the memory of that generation forever. Cui said he just wrote a love song without too much expectation. However, this song has been given much more implication as the time goes on. It has become the mark of an era.

三《让世界充满爱》

Ràng Shìjiè Chōngmǎn Ài

 Sing Together

群星 演唱

陈哲、小林、王健、郭峰、孙名 词

郭峰 曲

1. 轻轻地捧着你的脸, 为你把眼泪擦干。
2. 深深地凝望你的眼, 不需要更多的语言。

这颗心永远属于你, 告诉我不再孤单。
紧紧地握住你的手, 这温暖依旧未改变。

我们同欢乐, 我们同忍受, 我们怀着同样的期待。

我们共风雨, 我们共追求, 我们珍存同一样的爱。

无论你我可曾相识, 无论在眼前在天边,

真心地为你祝愿, 祝愿你幸福平安!

Qīngqīng de pěngzhe nǐ de liǎn,
轻轻　　地　捧着　你　的　脸，

wèi nǐ bǎ yǎnlèi cāgān.
为　你　把　眼泪　擦干。

Zhè kē xīn yǒngyuǎn shǔyú nǐ,
这　颗　心　永远　　属于　你，

gàosu wǒ bú zài gūdān.
告诉　我　不　再　孤单。

Shēnshēn de níngwàng nǐ de yǎn,
深深　　地　凝望　你　的　眼，

Bù xūyào gèng duō de yǔyán.
不　需要　更　多　的　语言。

Jǐnjǐn de wòzhù nǐ de shǒu,
紧紧　地　握住　你　的　手，

zhè wēnnuǎn yījiù wèi gǎibiàn.
这　温暖　依旧　未　改变。

Wǒmen tóng huānlè,
我们　同　欢乐，

wǒmen tóng rěnshòu,
我们　同　忍受，

wǒmen huáizhe tóngyàng de qīdài.
我们　怀着　同样　的　期待。

Wǒmen tóng fēngyǔ,
我们　同　风雨，

wǒmen gòng zhuīqiú,

我们　　共　追求，

wǒmen zhēncún tóng yí yàng de ài.

我们　珍存 同 一 样 的 爱。

Wúlùn nǐ wǒ kě céng xiāngshí,

无论　你 我 可 曾　相识，

wúlùn zài yǎnqián zài tiānbiān,

无论 在　眼前 在　天边，

zhēnxīn de wèi nǐ zhùyuàn,

真心　地 为 你　祝愿，

zhùyuàn nǐ xìngfú píng'ān!

祝愿　你 幸福　平安！

这首歌描写了对人类博爱的渴望。

我们生活在这个世界上，人与人之间需要爱。为悲伤的人擦去泪水，用同情之心安慰他，用援助之手温暖他。人类是一个集体，爱把我们联结在一起，风雨同舟、患难与共。无论是否相识，无论身在何方，祝愿所有的人幸福平安。

This song expresses the longing for universal love for mankind.

Living on this planet, we need love from each other. Let us wipe off the tears of grief, comfort them with sympathy, and warm their hearts with our helping hands. We are all connected by love and should share joys and sorrows together. Wish you a peaceful and happy life no matter where you are.

▶▶ 歌中词语　Vocabuary

1. 充满	chōngmǎn	to fill with
2. 捧	pěng	to hold or offer with both hands
3. 擦干	cāgān	to wipe sth. dry
4. 属于	shǔyú	to belong to
5. 不再	bú zài	no longer
6. 孤单	gūdān	lonely
7. 深深地	shēnshēn de	deeply
8. 凝望	níngwàng	to gaze
9. 紧紧地	jǐnjǐn de	tightly
10. 握	wò	to hold
11. 依旧	yījiù	still
12. 未	wèi	not
13. 忍受	rěnshòu	to endure
14. 怀着	huáizhe	to keep in mind
15. 期待	qīdài	to look forward to
16. 珍存	zhēncún	to treasure and keep
17. 相识	xiāngshí	to be acquainted with each other
18. 祝愿	zhùyuàn	to wish
19. 平安	píng'ān	safe and sound

1．让世界充满爱

"让"在这里是动词，表示愿望。多用于书面。

"让" is a verb here indicating the speaker's desire. It is usually used in the written language.

例如：让我们永远记住这件事。

让孩子们有一个快乐的童年。

2．握住你的手

"动+住"在这里表示牢固、稳固。

"Verb+住" here indicates the firm and solid state after an action is finished.

例如：请记住我的电话号码。

小男孩儿捉住了一只小鸟。

3．同欢乐／同忍受／同风雨／共追求

"同／共+动／形"用法中，"同"和"共"都是副词，意思是"一起"。多用于书面。

In "同／共+Verb／Adj.", "同" and "共" are both adverbs meaning "together" and are usually used in the written language.

例如：正好，我们同行。

我们同住一个房间。

4. 珍存同一样的爱

"同一样"，歌词中为了配合旋律的特殊用法，就是"同样"、"一样"。

"同一样" means "the same" ("同样"、"一样"). "一" is used to match the rhythm of the song.

5. 无论你我可曾相识

"无论"是连词，和"都"、"也"连用，表示在任何条件下结果都不会改变。在这里单独使用，是歌词中特殊用法。

"无论" is a conjunction usually used together with "都" or "也", indicating that no matter under what circumstances the result will remain the same. Here it is used alone as a special way of wording in lyrics.

> 例如：无论做什么工作，他都非常认真。
> 无论是谁，都要遵守纪律。

"可曾"常出现在诗歌、散文中。"可"是副词，用在问句中，加强语气，意思是"是否"。"曾"，就是"曾经"，表示发生过。

"可曾" is usually used in the poems and prose. "可" is an adverb often used in a question to emphasize the mood, meaning "是否"(have you ... or not?). "曾" means "ever" indicating that the action happened in the past.

> 例如：你可曾记得我们第一次见面？
> 你可曾知道，我为了你的事，跑过多少回？

歌手
About the Singer

郭峰（Guo Feng）

1962年出生于四川成都一个艺术之家，3岁学钢琴，14岁发表第一首作品。1986年为纪念国际和平年创作《让世界充满爱》，是第一首中国内地原创流行歌曲，成为内地流行音乐兴起的标志，郭峰因此被称为"中国流行音乐第一人"、"中国原创音乐开路人"。

从"音乐神童"到词曲创作、编曲、制作、演奏、演唱、策划、导演集于一身的全方位音乐人，"爱、友谊、和平"永远是郭峰创作的主题。他将音乐融入公益事业，多年来为许多大型公益活动创作歌曲，作品旋律优美、气势宏大，配器手法新颖，充满激情。

2000年，郭峰发起并组织了由奥申委批准并认可的"我为申奥万里歌"全国个人巡回公益演唱会。他还将为2008年北京奥运会创作一部大型组歌。目前，一个"环球音乐圣火传递"活动也正在筹备，郭峰希望用音乐把中国人支持奥运的精神传递给世界。

代表作：《让世界充满爱》《地球的孩子》《有你有我》《年轻的心》等。

Guo Feng was born into an artistic family in Chengdu, Sichuan Province in 1962. He started to learn to play piano at the age of three, and had his first opus published at 14. In 1986, he composed "Let the World Filled with Love" to commemorate the Year of the World Peace, which was the first piece of original popular song of mainland China and the mark of the rise of pop music in the mainland. Thus he is called "the first man of Chinese pop music", and "the trailblazer of Chinese original music".

From a "music wunderkind" to a versatile musician who does composing, lyric writing, producing, performing, singing, planning and directing, "love, friendship and peace" are always Guo's main themes. He connects music with public welfare, and has written songs for many major public welfare activities. His music has beautiful melodies, grand vigor, novel arrangement, and is full of passion.

In 2000, Guo initiated and organized a personal vocal concert tour nationwide, the "Long March Singing for Olympic Bidding", for public welfare, which was approved by the Olympic Games Bidding Committee. Furthermore, he is going to write a suite of songs for 2008 Beijing Olympic Games. Now, an activity called "Worldwide Music Torch Relay" is under preparation. Guo hopes that music will pass China's passion for supporting Olympic Games to the whole world.

Representative Songs: "Let the World Filled with Love", "Children of the Earth", "Along With You and Me", "Youthful Heart".

《让世界充满爱》问世已经20年了，如果它的旋律响起，我们周围百分之八十的人都会跟着哼唱。这是郭峰的成名作，也是留在人们心底的一首歌。

20世纪80年代初，人们认为流行歌曲只能表达风花雪月的小情调，根本无法表达有内涵的大主题。年轻的郭峰暗下决心要改变这种偏见。当时，围绕国际和平年这个主题，在美国，有《We Are the World》；在港台，有《明天会更好》，都由群星演唱。受到他们的启发，郭峰创作了由三首歌曲组成的《让世界充满爱》，并成功组织了一台同名演唱会，由内地百名歌星同台演出。

这首歌很快唱红了大江南北，人们听到了内地自己的流行歌曲，也知道了流行音乐同样能够承担重大的社会责任。简洁流畅的旋律、温暖动人的词句、歌词里第一次出现的"爱"这个字，印在了人们心里，也成为了郭峰的标记。

"Let the World Filled with Love" has been born for 20 years. When the melody starts, eighty percent of people would follow it. It's made Guo's name and still echoes in people's hearts.

In 1980s, people thought that pop songs only expressed romantic sentiment, and had nothing to do with great or important themes. As a young man, Guo was determined to change such prejudice. At that time, on the topic of the Year of the World Peace, there were the songs "We Are the World" in US and "Tomorrow Will Be Better" in Hong Kong and Taiwan, both sung by star singers. Inspired by these songs, Guo wrote "Let the World Filled with Love" consisted of three songs, and successfully conducted a vocal concert of the same title, with one hundred star singers from the mainland performing together on one stage.

This song has spread across the country and people in the mainland now have their own pop songs.They start to realize that pop music can also bear important social responsibility. Succinct and flowing melody, warm and touching words and the first appearing of the word "love" in lyrics impressed people deeply, which also became the sign of Guo Feng.

四 《甜蜜蜜》 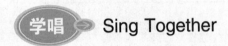 Tiánmìmì

学唱 Sing Together

邓丽君　演唱
庄奴　　词
汤妮　　曲

甜蜜　蜜，你笑得甜蜜蜜，　好像花儿

开在春风里，开在春风　里。

在哪里，在哪里见过你？　你的笑容

这样熟悉，我一时想不起。

啊！　在梦里。　梦里

梦里见过你，　　甜蜜笑得多甜

蜜。　　　是　你！　是　你！　梦　见　的　就　是

你！　　　在　哪　里，在　哪　里见过　你？

你的笑容　这样熟　　悉，我　一　时想不　起。

啊！　　　在　梦　　里。

歌词 Lyrics

Tiánmìmì,

甜蜜蜜，

nǐ xiào de tiánmìmì,

你 笑 得 甜蜜蜜，

hǎoxiàng huā'ér kāi zài chūnfēng li,

好像 花儿 开 在 春风 里，

kāi zài chūnfēng li.

开 在 春风 里。

Zài nǎli,

在 哪里，

zài nǎli jiànguo nǐ?

在 哪里 见过 你？

Nǐ de xiàoróng zhèyàng shúxī,
你 的 笑容 这样 熟悉，

wǒ yìshí xiǎng bu qǐ.
我 一时 想 不 起。

Ā! Zài mèng li.
啊！在 梦 里。

Mèng li mèng li jiànguo nǐ,
梦 里 梦 里 见过 你，

tiánmì xiào de duō tiánmì.
甜蜜 笑 得 多 甜蜜。

Shì nǐ! Shì nǐ!
是 你！是 你！

Mèngjiàn de jiùshì nǐ!
梦见 的 就是 你！

●●● 歌词大意 Main Idea of the Lyrics ●●●

这是一首甜蜜的情歌，描写一见钟情的情景。

心爱的人脸上的笑容比蜜糖还要甜，像春风中摇摆的花朵那样美丽。这迷人的笑容多么熟悉，好像在哪里见过？我一下子想不起来。对了，是在梦里！原来你就是我梦中的情人啊！

This is a sweet love song describing a scene in which a boy and a girl are falling in love at the first sight.

The smile on the face of the lover is sweeter than honey and as beautiful as the flowers dancing in the spring breeze. This charming smile is so familiar as if I have seen it somewhere. I can't remember it. Oh, it's in the dream! You are just the lover in my dream!

1. 甜蜜蜜	tiánmìmì	sweet，happy
2. 开	kāi	to bloom
3. 春风	chūnfēng	spring breeze
4. 笑容	xiàoróng	smiling face
5. 熟悉	shúxī	familiar
6. 一时	yìshí	momentary
7. 梦见	mèngjiàn	to dream of

▶▶ 歌中句式   Grammer Notes

1. 甜蜜蜜

"甜蜜蜜"是"甜"的生动形式。汉语中很多形容词可以重叠，使表达的意义更加生动。有"AA+BB"、"A+BB"等形式。

"甜蜜蜜" is the lively form of "甜". A lot of adjectives can be reduplicated to convey the vivid meaning. The common form is "AA+BB" or "A+BB".

例如：漂亮——漂漂亮亮
      清楚——清清楚楚
      绿——绿油油
      喜——喜洋洋

2. 笑得**多**甜蜜

"动+得+多+形"表示感叹。"多"是副词，表示程度很高。"多+形"对前面的动词进行补充修饰。

"V+得+多+Adj." forms an exclamatory sentence. "多" is an adverb indicating that the degree is very high. "多+adj." modifies the previous verb.

例如：孩子们玩得多高兴啊！
　　　昨天雨下得多大啊！

3. 开**在**春风里

由"在"组成的介词结构有时可以放在动词后面。
The preposition phrase with "在" sometimes is put after the verb.

例如：照片挂在墙上。
　　　阳光洒在房间里。

4. 想**不起**

"动+不+起"的句式，表示能力等达不到某种要求或目的。

The structure "verb +不+起" indicates that being unable to meet the requirement or achieve the objective.

例如：房子太贵了，年轻人买不起。
　　　他说五年后结婚，可是我等不起。

5. 梦见的就是你

梦见的(人)，"动+的（+名）"是"的"字短语，用来代替名词。

The "的" phrase "V+的 (+N)" refers to the noun after "的" which is omitted.

例如：天太热，游泳的（人）很多。
过去的（事情）就忘了吧！

歌手
About the Singer

邓丽君 (Teresa Teng)

　　祖籍河北，1953 年 1 月生于台湾，1995 年 5 月在泰国清迈去世。邓丽君拥有超凡的演唱天赋，14 岁休学，正式以歌唱为职业。她的声音甜美柔和，演唱技巧完美，充满感染力，被称为"一代歌后"，在华语流行乐坛的地位至今无人超越。

　　邓丽君的音乐代表了 20 世纪 70 年代中期至 80 年代初期亚洲流行音乐的较高水平，对华语乐坛、日本乐坛都有不凡影响，特别是对中国内地的流行歌手、音乐人影响巨大，对内地流行音乐的早期开发具有启蒙作用。

　　在流行乐史上，邓丽君是最能代表华人社会的女歌手，只要是有华人的地方，就有她那充满乡情乡韵的歌声。她的作品融合了多种民族民间乐风和西方流行音乐的表现手段，小调式的中国旋律，曲调委婉动人，令人无法忘怀。

　　代表作：《甜蜜蜜》《小城故事》《我只在乎你》《月亮代表我的心》等。

Teresa Teng, whose ancestral home is in Hebei Province, was born in Taiwan in Jan. 1953, and died in Chiengmai, Thailand in May, 1995. Teng was extraordinarily talented in singing. She suspended her schooling at 14 years old and began her singing career. She was called "the singing queen of a generation" because of her sweet and soft voice and perfect singing skill, which were extremely infectious. Till now nobody has exceeded her in the Chinese pop musical circle.

Teresa Teng's songs represent the high level of Asian pop music between mid 70s to early of 80s. Her music had been making considerable influence on the Chinese and Japanese pop musical circles, especially to the pop singers and musicians from China's mainland. What's more, her songs enlightened the early-stage exploitation of pop music in the mainland.

In the history of pop music, Teresa Teng is the most representative songstress of the Chinese society. Her nostalgic melodies spread everywhere Chinese people live. Integrating the musical styles of many Chinese folk groups and the expressive techniques of Western pop music, Teng brought us unforgettable canzonet-like Chinese melodies that linger for generations.

Representative Songs: "Your Sweet Smiles", "Small Town Story", "I Only Care about You", "The Moon Represents My Heart".

作者
About the Writer

《甜蜜蜜》的词作者庄奴，是台湾的"词坛泰斗"。1921 年生于北京，1949 年到台湾。一次，他的词《绿岛小夜曲》被人谱曲后，竟然非常流行，从此他便开始专业写歌词。50 多年来，庄奴写了 3000 多首歌词，成为华语流行乐坛的一个奇迹。他和内地的乔羽、香港的黄霑并称"词坛三杰"。

有人说"没有庄奴，就没有邓丽君。"因为邓丽君演唱的歌曲中，百分之八十出自庄奴。老先生回忆，他们的合作始于《甜蜜蜜》。当年有人拿着乐谱来找他填词，一问才知道要唱这首歌的人是邓丽君，于是他的眼前一下子浮现出邓丽君那张圆圆的脸、甜甜的说话声和甜甜的歌声，立刻想起了"甜蜜蜜"这个词，于是，五分钟就完成了这首歌词。

1997 年，《甜蜜蜜》这首歌再度风靡，原因是同名电影的上映。这部电影的主演是黎明和张曼玉，讲述了一个曲折的爱情故事，从头到尾贯穿着《甜蜜蜜》这首歌。本片在香港电影"金像奖"评选中，破纪录地夺得了九项大奖。

The lyric writer of "Your Sweet Smiles" is Zhuang Nu, regarded as the leader of the lyric circle in Taiwan. He was born in Beijing in 1921 and went to Taiwan in 1949. After his lyrics of "Green Island Serenade" became unexpectedly popular, he began to take lyrics writing as a profession. During the period of 50-odd years, Zhuang Nu has written more than 3,000 pieces of songs, which was considered as a miracle in the history of Chinese pop music. He is regarded as one of "the three elitists in lyrics writing", with Qiao Yu from the mainland and Huang Zhan from Hongkong being the other two.

Eighty percent of Teresa Teng's songs were produced by Zhuang Nu, from which some people drew the conclusion that "Teresa Teng owed her popularity to Zhuang Nu." Mr. Zhuang recalled their first cooperation starting with "Your Sweet Smiles". When he was invited to write the lyrics for a musical composition and was told the singer would be Teresa Teng, he seemed to see her sweet image and hear her sweet voice immediately. The words "Your Sweet Smiles" jumped into his mind and he accomplished the lyrics in five minutes.

In 1997, due to the show of the film with the same title, this song became a hit again. Starred by Leon Lai and Maggie Cheung Man-yuk, the film is about a romantic love story with this song's accompany from the beginning to the end. The film won 9 awards of Hong Kong Film Awards, which broke the record.

五《童年》Tóngnián

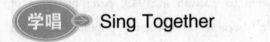

学唱 ⇨ Sing Together

罗大佑　演唱

罗大佑　词曲

（乐谱）

1. 池塘边的榕树上，知了在声声叫着夏天，
2. 福利社里面，什么都有，就是口袋里没有半毛钱，
3. 总是要等到睡觉前，才知道功课只做了一点点，
4. 没有人知道为什么，太阳总下到山的那一边，
5. 阳光下蜻蜓飞过来，一片片绿油油的稻田，

操场边的秋千上，只有蝴蝶停在上面，
黑板上老师的粉笔，还在拼命叽叽喳喳写个不停，
等待着下课，等待着放学，等待游戏的童年，
总是要等到考试以后，才知道该念的书都没有念，
一寸光阴一寸金，老师说过寸金难买寸光阴，

盼望着假期，盼望着明天，盼望长大的童年。

写 不 停。
我 个 窗 前?
寸 的 光 阴。
天 空 发 呆。
长 大 的 脸。

等 待 着 着 下 零 一 好 假 课， 食 天 奇 期，
待 里 天 这 的 零 好 一 假 食 天 奇
心 迷 这 望 游 戏 的 童 童 童 年。年。年。年。年。
等 待 着 着 手 一 就 盼

等 待 着 着 学，放 漫 一 幻 明
待 里 年 这 着 的 又 么 望 画 想 天，
等 心 迷 这 望 恋 初 糊 孤 长
手 一 就 盼 游 戏 的 的 的 的 单 大

歌词 · Lyrics

Chítáng biān de róngshù shang,
池塘　　边的　榕树　　上，

zhīliǎo zài shēngshēng de jiàozhe xiàtiān.
知了　在　　声声　地　叫着　夏天。

Cāochǎng biān de qiūqiān shang,
操场　　边的　秋千　上，

zhǐyǒu húdiér tíng zài shàngmian.
只有　蝴蝶儿　停在　上面。

Hēibǎn shang lǎoshī de fěnbǐ,
黑板　上　老师　的　粉笔，

hái zài pīnmìng jījizhāzhā xiě ge bù tíng.
还在　拼命　叩叩喳喳　写个　不　停。

Děngdàizhe xiàkè,
等待着　下课，

děngdàizhe fàngxué,
等待着　　放学，

děngdài yóuxì de tóngnián.
等待 游戏 的 童年。

Fúlìshè lǐmian shénme dōu yǒu,
福利社 里面 什么 都 有,

jiùshì kǒudai li méiyǒu bàn máo qián.
就是 口袋 里 没有 半 毛 钱。

Zhūgě sì láng hé móguǐdǎng,
诸葛 四 郎 和 魔鬼党,

dàodǐ shuí qiǎngdào nà zhī bǎojiàn?
到底 谁 抢到 那 支 宝剑?

Gébì bān de nàge nǚhái,
隔壁 班 的 那个 女孩,

zěnme hái méi jīngguò wǒ de chuāng qián?
怎么 还 没 经过 我 的 窗 前?

Zuǐ li de língshí,
嘴 里 的 零食,

shǒu li de mànhuà,
手 里 的 漫画,

xīn li chūliàn de tóngnián.
心 里 初恋 的 童年。

Zǒngshì yào děngdào shuìjiào qián,
总是 要 等到 睡觉 前,

cái zhīdào gōngkè zhǐ zuòliǎo yìdiǎndiǎn.
才 知道 功课 只 做了 一点点。

Zǒngshì yào děngdào kǎoshì yǐhòu,
总是 要 等到 考试 以后,

cái zhīdào gāi niàn de shū dōu méiyǒu niàn.
才 知道 该 念 的 书 都 没有 念。

Yí cùn guāngyīn yí cùn jīn,
一 寸 光阴 一 寸 金,

lǎoshī shuōguo cùn jīn nán mǎi cùn guāngyīn.
老师 说过 寸 金 难 买 寸 光阴。

Yì tiān yòu yì tiān,
一 天 又 一 天,

yì nián yòu yì nián,
一 年 又 一 年,

mímihūhū de tóngnián.
迷迷糊糊 的 童年。

Méiyǒu rén zhīdào wèishénme,
没有 人 知道 为什么,

tàiyáng zǒng xiàdao shān de nà yì biān.
太阳 总 下到 山 的 那 一 边。

Méiyǒu rén nénggòu gàosu wǒ,
没有 人 能够 告诉 我,

shān lǐmian yǒu méiyǒu zhùzhe shénxiān.
山 里面 有 没有 住着 神仙。

Duōshǎo de rìzi li,
多少 的 日子 里,

zǒngshì yí gè rén miànduìzhe tiānkōng fādāi.
总是 一 个 人 面对着 天空 发呆。

Jiù zhème hàoqí,
就 这么 好奇,

jiù zhème huànxiǎng,
就 这么 幻想,

zhème gūdān de tóngnián.
这么　　孤单　的　　童年。

Yángguāng xià qīngtíng fēi guolai,
阳光　　　下　蜻蜓　飞　过来，

yípiànpiàn lǜyóuyóu de dàotián.
一片片　　绿油油　的　稻田。

Shuǐcǎi làbǐ hé wànhuātǒng,
水彩　蜡笔　和　万花筒，

huà bu chū tiānbiān nà yí dào cǎihóng.
画　不　出　天边　那　一　道　彩虹。

Shénme shíhou cáinéng xiàng gāo niánjí de tóngxué,
什么　　时候　才能　像　高　年级　的　同学，

yǒu zhāng chéngshú yǔ zhǎngdà de liǎn.
有　张　　成熟　　与　长大　的　脸。

Pànwàngzhe jiàqī,
盼望着　　假期，

pànwàngzhe míngtiān,
盼望着　　明天，

pànwàng zhǎngdà de tóngnián.
盼望　　长大　的　童年。

Ō, yì tiān yòu yì tiān,
噢，一　天　又　一　天，

yì nián yòu yì nián,
一　年　又　一　年，

pànwàng zhǎngdà de tóngnián.
盼望　　长大　的　童年。

歌词大意 Main Idea of the Lyrics ●●●

这首歌写的是你我共同的"童年"，每个人在成长过程中都经历过的那些稚嫩的小小心思，是多么有趣而又可爱。

我们坐在教室里，心早已飞到了窗外，盼着早点儿下课。老师说过要珍惜时间，可是我们总是玩不够。功课没做完，考试考不好，怎么办呢？每天如果看不到隔壁班的那个女孩，就会很失望。心里常常有很多问题，可是没人告诉我们答案，只好自己想一想。快点放假吧！过了假期，就长大一岁。长大了，一切就都好了。

This song depicts the happy childhood cherished by everyone of us. We all grew up with those little childish and naive secrets. How interesting and lovely they were!

We were sitting in the classroom, but our mind had already flown out of the window, longing for the class to be dismissed. The teacher told us to cherish the time, but we could never have enough time to play. There were always unfinished assignments and poor scores of tests. What should we do? I wanted to have a look at the girl in the next classroom everyday, otherwise I would get very disappointed. There were many questions in our minds, but nobody gave us the answers and we had to think of them ourselves. How I wished an early arrival of the vacation! After it, I'd be one year older and everything would be fine.

▶▶ 歌中词语　　Vocabuary

1.	池塘	chítáng	pond
2.	榕树	róngshù	banyan
3.	知了	zhīliǎo	cicada
4.	秋千	qiūqiān	swing
5.	蝴蝶	húdié	butterfly
6.	拼命	pīnmìng	with all one's might
7.	叽叽喳喳	jījizhāzhā	to chirp
8.	游戏	yóuxì	to play; game
9.	福利社	fúlìshè	buffet, canteen
10.	口袋	kǒudai	pockets
11.	到底	dàodǐ	on earth
12.	抢	qiǎng	to rob
13.	宝剑	bǎojiàn	sword
14.	隔壁	gébì	neighbour, next door
15.	经过	jīngguò	pass by
16.	零食	língshí	snack
17.	漫画	mànhuà	cartoon
18.	初恋	chūliàn	first love
19.	功课	gōngkè	school assignment
20.	念(书)	niàn (shū)	study
21.	迷迷糊糊	mímihūhū	be in a daze
22.	下(山)	xià (shān)	(of the sun) set

23. 神仙	shénxiān	immortal
24. 面对	miànduì	to face
25. 发呆	fādāi	stare blankly
26. 好奇	hàoqí	curious
27. 幻想	huànxiǎng	to fancy
28. 蜻蜓	qīngtíng	dragonfly
29. 绿油油	lǜyóuyóu	lush green
30. 稻田	dàotián	rice field
31. 水彩	shuǐcǎi	watercolor
32. 蜡笔	làbǐ	crayon
33. 万花筒	wànhuātǒng	kaleidoscope
34. 彩虹	cǎihóng	rainbow
35. 成熟	chéngshú	mature
36. 盼望	pànwàng	to look forward to

 **Grammer Notes**

1. 福利社里什么都有

"什么"用在"都、也"前，表示在所说的范围内无例外。

"什么"in front of "都、也" indicates that all is included in the range with no exception.

例如：我去超市，什么都想买。

我感冒了，什么也吃不下。

2. 就是口袋里没有半毛钱

"就是"在这里意思是"只是"。

"就是" here means "只是" (just).

例如：他的汉语挺好的，就是发音还需要练习。

这里的冬天不太冷，就是有点儿干燥。

3. 诸葛四郎和魔鬼党

这是漫画故事里的人物。他们为了得到一支神奇的剑而打斗。

These two are the characters in the cartoon who, fight for a magic sword.

4. 总是要等到睡觉以前，才知道功课只做了一点点／太阳总下到山的那一边

"总(+是)+动"表示持续不变。

"总(+是)+Verb" means "always".

例如：他总是最后一个离开办公室。

我总去那家小饭馆吃面条。

"才"在时间词后，表示说话人认为事情发生的时间晚或历时久。

"才" is used after the time word to indicate that the speaker thinks the action is finished too late or takes too long.

例如：刘林每天晚上十点才下班。
　　　我叫了好几次，他才来。

5. 一寸光阴一寸金，寸金难买寸光阴

时间像黄金一样宝贵，但你有黄金也买不来时间。"寸"，中国的长度单位。"光阴"，时间。

Time is as valuable as the gold but you can not buy time with gold. "寸" is a Chinese measure word for length. "光阴" means time.

6. 一天又一天，一年又一年

"又"前后重复同一"一+量"，表示反复多次。

"又" between two "一+Measure word" indicates the repetition of many times.

例如：同学们一次又一次地练习。
　　　一批又一批的留学生来这里学习。

7. 阳光下蜻蜓飞过来

"动+过来(+名)"表示人或事物随动作从一处到另一处。

"Verb+过来 (+Noun)" indicates that the person or something follows the action from one place to another.

例如：一位老人慢慢走过来。
　　　远处跑过来一只小狗。

8. 画不出天边那一道彩虹

"动+出（+名）"表示人或事物随动作从里向外。否定式在"出"前加"不"。

"Verb+出 (+Noun)" indicates that the person or something follows the action from inside to outside. The negative is formed by putting "不" in front of "出".

例如：我激动得说不出话。

树林里跳出一只小鹿。

歌手
About the Singer

罗大佑 (Lo Ta Yu)

1954 年 7 月生于台北。为音乐放弃医生工作，20 多年的创作对华语流行乐坛意义非凡，人称"音乐教父"。

他的一部分歌曲对社会现状进行反思、批判，思想深刻，影响巨大，被评价为"中国的 Bob Dylan"、"抗议歌手"、"愤怒青年"；然而，他还有"情歌圣手"的称号，情歌是他作品中非常重要的一部分。犀利敏锐和温情细腻构成了罗大佑的永恒魅力。

罗大佑的歌声伴随了几代人的成长。2000 年 9 月罗大佑首次在内地开演唱会，充分展示了他"华语乐坛精神偶像"的力量。全国各地歌迷聚集上海，北京歌迷就有上千名。能容纳八万人的体育场里，数万名三四十岁的人用歌声与泪水见证了逝去的青春。

2005 年，罗大佑的《现象七十二变》被收入中国高等教育出版社新版《大学语文》课本的诗歌篇。罗大佑歌曲的价值在一个新的层面上得到了承认。

代表作：《童年》《光阴的故事》《鹿港小镇》《东方之珠》等。

Lo Ta Yu was born in Taipei in July 1954. When he was young, he quitted the career as a doctor and embarked on the career of music. During his over 20 years' music he has made extraordinary contribution to the Chinese pop music and is therefore given the title of "godfather of Chinese music".

Lo infuses his witty commentary on social and political issues in his songs and is thus considered "Chinese Bob Dylan", "a protestant singer", and "an angry young man". However, he also has the title of "master of love songs" for the great number of popular love songs he has produced. It is his incisiveness, acuity, tenderness and exquisiteness that have made Lo's everlasting charm.

Lo's songs have accompanied the growth of several generations. In September 2000, Lo Ta Yu held his first concert in the mainland. As a major cultural icon in the Chinese pop musical circle, Lo showed his charm in front of his fans from all over the country gathering in Shanghai, and among them there were over a thousand coming from Beijing. In the stadium which can hold 80,000 people, tens of thousands of people in their thirties and forties relived their passing youth in melodies with tears.

In 2005, Lo's "72 Transformations" was included in the verse section of the new edition of *College Chinese* published by China's Higher Education Press, which indicates that Lo's songs have been acknowledg at a new level.

Representative Songs: "Childhood", "Story of Time", "The Little Town Lugang", "Pearl of the Orient".

20世纪80年代中期，许多内地的年轻人就是听了这首歌，知道了罗大佑的名字。无忧无虑的童年是所有人共同的回忆，《童年》这首抒写罗大佑童年情怀的歌，也就成了大家歌唱自己童年的歌。

罗大佑出生在一个医生家庭。由于父亲工作的缘故，罗大佑在城市和乡村都生活过。"五岁的时候，我们全家搬到宜兰。……虽然只有一年半，宜兰却是我后来创作《童年》这首歌里的重要场景。……里面只有池塘是我搬过来的，其他的场景都一模一样。"童年时，他也是个贪玩儿的孩子，后来读书十几年，考试无数次，让他更加怀念儿时的快乐生活。于是，罗大佑在医大读书期间，足足花了五年时间，平均一段歌词一年，终于成就了这首经典之作——《童年》。

In mid of 1980's, many young people got to know Lo Ta Yu through the song "Childhood". Happy childhood is the common memory of all people and they sing "Childhood" to cherish that period of carefree time.

Lo Ta Yu was born to a doctor's family. Due to his father's work, he had the chance to live in both urban and rural areas. " When I was five years old, my family moved to Yilan where we spent one year and a half. The important scenes in 'Childhood' all came from this place, except the pool that I moved there." In his carefree childhood, Lo was a naughty boy who enjoyed playing around all day. During the following over 10 years of schooling he had to take countless examinations, which made him cherish his happy childhood even more. The song was created while Lo was in the medical school. He spent five years to finish the lyrics, one segment in each year on average, and finally finished this classical song that has captivated the hearts of generations.

六《大约在冬季》

Dàyuē zài Dōngjì

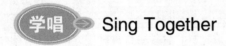

学唱 → Sing Together

齐 秦 演唱
齐 秦 词曲

轻轻地， 我将离开你， 请将眼角的泪拭去。 漫漫

长夜里，未来日子里，亲爱的你别为我哭泣。

前方的路虽然太凄迷，请在笑容里为我祝福。 虽然

迎着风， 虽然下着雨，我在 风雨之中念着你。

没有你的日子里，我会更加珍惜自己；

没有我的岁月里，你要保重你自己。

你问我，何时归故里，我也 轻声地问自己。 不是

在此时，不知在何时，我想 大约会是在冬季。 不是

在此时，不知在何时，我想 大约会是在冬季。

大约会是在冬季，不是 在此时，不知在何时，我想

大约会是在 冬 季。

歌词 Lyrics

Qīngqīng de, wǒ jiāng líkāi nǐ,
轻轻 地，我 将 离开 你，

qǐng jiāng yǎnjiǎo de lèi shìqù.
请 将 眼角 的 泪 拭去。

Mànmàn chángyè li, wèilái rìzi li,
漫漫 长夜 里，未来 日子 里，

qīnài de, nǐ bié wèi wǒ kūqì.
亲爱 的，你 别 为 我 哭泣。

Qiánfāng de lù suīrán tài qīmí,
前方 的 路 虽然 太 凄迷，

qǐng zài xiàoróng li wèi wǒ zhùfú.
请 在 笑容 里 为 我 祝福。

Suīrán yíngzhe fēng, suīrán xiàzhe yǔ,
虽然 迎着 风, 虽然 下着 雨,

wǒ zài fēngyǔ zhīzhōng niànzhe nǐ.
我 在 风雨 之中 念着 你。

Méiyǒu nǐ de rìzi li,
没有 你 的 日子里,

wǒ huì gèngjiā zhēnxī zìjǐ;
我 会 更加 珍惜 自己;

méiyǒu wǒ de suìyuè li,
没有 我 的 岁月里,

nǐ yào bǎozhòng nǐ zìjǐ.
你 要 保重 你 自己。

Nǐ wèn wǒ, héshí guī gùlǐ,
你 问 我, 何时 归 故里,

wǒ yě qīngshēng de wèn zìjǐ.
我 也 轻声 地 问 自己。

Bú shì zài cǐshí, bù zhī zài héshí,
不 是 在 此时, 不 知 在 何时,

wǒ xiǎng dàyuē huì shì zài dōngjì.
我 想 大约 会 是 在 冬季。

●●● 歌词大意 Main Idea of the Lyrics ●●●

这是一首情人离别时的歌，有一种淡淡的忧伤。

我要离开你去远方，未来的路漫长且充满未知，但是亲爱的，别哭，微笑着祝福我吧！无论前路怎样艰险，我都会思念你。在我们天各一方的日子里，你我要珍重自己。虽然我不知道什么时候回来，但我希望在一个寒冷的冬季，我们会有一个温暖的相聚。

This melancholy song describes the scene of the parting of two lovers.

I will leave you and go far away. The road to the future is long and full of uncertainty. But don't cry, my dear. Wish me good luck with a smile! No matter how hard the journey ahead will be, I will miss you! While we are apart, we both should cherish ourselves. Though I am not sure when I can come back, I'll be looking forward to a warm reunion in a chilly winter.

1. 大约	dàyuē	probably
2. 眼角	yǎnjiǎo	corner of the eye
3. 拭(去)	shì(qù)	to wipe off
4. 漫漫	mànmàn	very long
5. 哭泣	kūqì	to weep
6. 前方	qiánfāng	ahead
7. 凄迷	qīmí	dreary and hazy
8. 祝福	zhùfú	to bless
9. 迎	yíng	to face
10. 念	niàn	to miss
11. 珍惜	zhēnxī	to cherish
12. 岁月	suìyuè	years, days
13. 保重	bǎozhòng	to take care of oneself
14. 归	guī	to go back
15. 故里	gùlǐ	native place, home town
16. 此时	cǐshí	now

▶▶ 歌中句式　Grammer Notes

1. 我将①离开你／请将②眼角的泪拭去

　　"将①"是时间副词，表示动作或情况不久就会发生。
"将②"是介词，意思是"把"。二者都用于书面语。
　　"将①", an adverb of time, indicates that something will

happen soon. "将②", a preposition, means "把". Both are used in written language.

例如：火车将①晚点。

五场比赛将①同时进行。

他将②文件交给了我。

我们一定将②问题调查清楚。

2. 漫漫长夜里 ／ 未来日子里

"名+里"表示时间。这里的名词主要是表示一段时间的词语。

"Noun + 里" indicates time. Nouns used here should be those indicating a period of time.

例如：日里思，夜里想。

假期里她什么都没做。

3. 别为我哭泣 ／ 为我祝福

"为+名+动"用法中"为"是介词，引出动作的对象，意思是"替"或"给"。

In the structure "为 (wèi) + Noun + Verb", "为 (wèi)" is a preposition introducing the object of action, meaning "替" or "给" ("for").

例如：不要为我担心。

我为老板工作。

4. 前方的路虽然太凄迷

"虽然"常和"但是"、"可是"、"却"等连用，说明乙事并不因为甲事而改变。在意思说清楚的情况下，不用"但是"等也可以。

"虽然" is commonly used together with "但是"、"可是"、"却" etc., indicating that situation A will not change because of situation B. If the context is clear enough, "虽然" alone can be used.

例如：天气虽然很热，教室里挺凉快的。

虽然我不知道你更多，我知道你是个好人。

5. 在风雨之中

"在+名+（之）中"表示一件事发生在另一件事的进程中。"之"可以省略。

"在 + Noun +（之） 中" indicates that one thing happens in the procedure of another thing. "之" can be omitted.

例如：在工作中我们要不断学习新知识。

他和她在劳动中相识、相爱。

6. 没有你的日子里 / 没有我的岁月里

"的"是助词，定语的标志。动词短语"没有你"、"没有我"是定语，限定中心语"日子"。

"的", a particle, is the mark of an attribute. Verb-phrase "没有你" and "没有我" are attributes to modify the nouns "日子" and "岁月".

例如：你买的书比较贵。

这是我写好的报告。

歌手
About the Singer

齐秦 (Chyi Chin)

　　祖籍辽宁，1960 年 1 月出生于台湾。1981 年至今，一直活跃在歌坛，是继邓丽君、刘文正之后，对内地影响最大的台湾音乐人之一，歌迷包括了 60、70、80 三个年代出生的人。1986 年，内地引进他的专辑《狼 I 》，引起轰动，不少歌手凭借演唱他的《大约在冬季》和《外面的世界》而扬名歌坛。如今这张唱片仍在畅销。

　　齐秦是一位天生的歌手，他嗓音高亢明亮、清澈飘逸，音乐与唱法非常个性化。齐秦创作并演唱的歌曲既有沧桑绝望的一面，又有温情甜蜜的一面，主题总围绕青春的失意与迷惘，以及年少时的爱情伤痛，因此成为无数人青春岁月的记忆载体。这一切使他独具魅力，加上他在音乐创作等方面一直不断前进着，因此，不仅在流行音乐史上留下了足迹，而且成为了歌坛常青树，至今都是媒体关注的焦点。

　　代表作：《狼》《大约在冬季》《外面的世界》《爱情宣言》《无情的雨，无情的你》等。

Chyi Chin, whose ancestral home is in Liaoning, was born in Taiwan in January 1960. Since 1981, he has been very active in the singing circle. Following Deng Lijun and Liu Wenzheng, he is one of the most influential Taiwanese singers in the mainland. His fans include people who were born in the sixties, seventies and eighties. In 1986, his album "Wolf I" was introduced to the mainland and made a great hit. Many singers became popular by singing his songs "Maybe in Winter" and "The World Outside". Today, this album is still very popular in the mainland.

Chyi Chin is a born singer with a voice sonorous and bright, clear and elegant. He has his own characteristics in musical style and expression. The songs created and sung by him have the element of desperation, as well as warmth and sweetness. With themes centering on the frustration and bewilderment of youth and the grief in love, his songs have become the memorial carrier for countless people to remember those days when they were young.

Despite the unique charm he has possessed, Chyi has never stopped in his pursuit of lyric writing and singing. He has not only left a footprint in the history of Chinese pop music but also become "the evergreen tree" in the musical circle. Up to now he is still the focus of the medium.

Representative Songs: "Wolf", "Maybe in Winter", "The World Outside", "The Love Declaration", "The Unmerciful Rain and Unmerciful You".

作者
About the Writer

　　齐秦有"情歌王子"之称，他以《狼》成名，但真正让他成为歌坛偶像的是他原创的"齐氏情歌"。《大约在冬季》是最早、最有代表性的一首，曾获 1988 年香港十大金曲奖。他与女友爱情长跑十几年，几次分分合合，最终分手。曲折的爱情经历，给他的情歌提供了无限的创作素材。

　　这首歌是齐秦专为女友所写的。有一次，他们要分别了，女友在熟睡，齐秦望着她，思绪万千，创作灵感闪现在脑海，《大约在冬季》就这样诞生了。因为现实中女友从没给过齐秦求婚的"结果"，所以他的情歌表达的都是对爱情的绝望和对结果的渴望，但又表现出男人对所爱女人的无限包容，这也正是"齐氏情歌"令人感动的原因所在。

Chyi Chin, with the title of "the prince of love songs", was mads popular by his "Wolf". However, what made him the real idol of the musical circle is his original "love songs of Qi's". "Maybe in Winter" is the earliest and most representative one, which won the prize of 1988's Top Ten Hong Kong Pop Songs Award. The love between him and his girlfriend lasted for over 10 years, with breaking-ups and reconciliations, and finally came to an end. The twists and turns in his love experience have provided him with measureless source materials for his love songs.

This song was specially written for his girlfriend when they would leave each other once. When his girlfriend was in a sound sleep, Chyi Chin looked at her with complicated feelings and thoughts, and the song "Maybe in Winter" was born. In reality, his girlfriend never accepted his proposal, hence all of his love songs express the desperation of love and the eagerness for the result. But he also shows how much a man can tolerate the woman he loves, which is the exact reason why Chyi Chin's love songs are so touching.

Focus 时代背景（一）
Background Information I

In early 80s an equipment called recorder began to change people's lives in China's mainland. Songs never heard before came out softly and sweetly from that black brick-like box. They were songs for love! Whoever listened to them felt he was melted in the melodies. That was Teresa Teng, the very first Hong Kongese and Taiwanese singing star who brought popular songs to the mainland. Before long, fresh and lovely campus songs from Taiwan came to the mainland, just like a morning breeze from the countryside.

In mid 80s, televisions entered ordinary Chinese families. The 9-inch black-and-white television brought tremendous happiness to the humdrum lives. In 1984, CCTV live broadcast their first Spring Festival Gala. From then on, people could see stars from Hong Kong and Taiwan on TV on New Year's Eve every year. The scene

80 年代初的中国内地，一种叫做录音机的东西开始改变人们的生活。黑色砖块模样的盒子里传出以前从没听过的歌声，软绵绵、甜蜜蜜，大胆地歌唱着爱情，听得整个人好像都要融化了。那就是邓丽君，第一位让人们听到"流行歌曲"的港台歌星。不久，清新动人的台湾校园歌曲，仿佛一阵清晨乡间的风，吹向了内地歌坛。

80 年代中期，电视走进普通家庭，九英寸黑白电视机为人们单调的生活又增添了无数欢乐。1984 年，中国中央电视台举办了第一次春节联欢晚会，从此，每年的除夕夜，人们都能在屏幕上欣赏来自香港、台湾的歌星演唱。十几个甚至几十个人聚集在一台电视机前观赏港台电视连续剧，成为那个年代文化生活的标记，电视剧插曲也由此加入了流行歌曲的行列。同时，电台节目中开始出现流行歌曲点播，这在当时真是一件新鲜事。

内地歌坛在这流行风的熏染中，从模仿到探索，歌手、词曲作者渐渐有了自己的风格。1986年是国际和平年，5月，百名内地歌星成功举办了《让世界充满爱》大型流行音乐演唱会，全面展示了内地流行音乐的实力，在中国流行音乐史上写下了一个大大的感叹号。这一年，流行音乐得到了官方和传媒的一致认可。全国青年歌手电视大奖赛第一次设置了"通俗唱法组"，从此中国内地歌坛开始有了美声、民族和通俗三种唱法。流行音乐终于正式登上了中国流行文化的主流舞台。

that dozens of people crowded in front of one TV set to watch the performance by Hong Kongese and Taiwanese star singers became a sign of that time. The theme songs in sitcoms become popular too. Pop songs of the cultural life were broadcast on request in radio programs, which was rather a novel phenomenon at that time.

Influenced by this popular trend, singers and composers in the mainland gradually developed their own styles from imitating to further exploring. In May, 1986, the Year of the World Peace, hundreds of singing stars successfully conducted a large-scale vocal concert, "Let the World Fiued with Love", which fully showed the strength of the pop music of the mainland, leaving a marvelous record in the history of Chinese pop music.

In the same year, pop music gained approval from both the authority and the media. After the National TV Singing Competition for Young Vocalists first set the "pop style" group in addition to bel canto and folk style, the pop music finally joined the mainstream of Chinese popular culture.

唱新歌 学汉语

SING SONGS AND
LEARN CHINESE

Pop Songs in the 90's
九十年代好歌

七《弯弯的月亮》

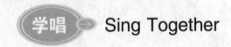
Wānwān de Yuèliang

学唱 Sing Together

刘 欢 演唱
李海鹰 词曲

1. 遥远的夜空, 有一个弯弯的月亮,
2. 阿娇摇着船, 唱着那古老的歌谣,

弯弯的月亮下面, 是那弯弯的小桥。

歌声随风飘, 飘到我的脸上。

小桥的旁边, 有一条弯弯的小船,
脸上淌着泪, 像那条弯弯的河水,

弯弯的小船悠悠, 是那童年的阿娇。
弯弯的河水流啊, 流进我的心上。

呜……我的心充满惆怅不为那弯弯的

月亮, 只为那今天的村庄,还唱着过去的

歌谣。　　呜……　　　故　乡　　的

月　亮，你那弯　　弯的忧　伤，穿　透了我的胸

膛。

Yáoyuǎn　de　yèkōng,
遥远　　　的　夜空，

yǒu　yí　ge　wānwān　de　yuèliàng,
有　一　个　弯弯　　的　月亮，

wānwān　de　yuèliàng　xiàmian,
弯弯　　的　月亮　　　下面，

shì　nà　wānwān　de　xiǎo　qiáo.
是　那　弯弯　　的　小　桥。

Xiǎo　qiáo　de　pángbiān,
小　桥　　的　旁边，

yǒu　yì　tiáo　wānwān　de　xiǎo　chuán,
有　一　条　弯弯　　的　小　船，

wānwān　de　xiǎo　chuán　yōuyōu,
弯弯　　的　小　船　　悠悠，

shì　nà　tóngnián　de　Ā　jiāo.
是　那　童年　　的　阿　娇。

Wū……
呜……

Ā jiāo yáozhe chuán,
阿娇 摇着 船，

chàngzhe nà gǔlǎo de gēyáo,
唱着 那 古老 的 歌谣，

gēshēng suí fēng piāo,
歌声 随 风 飘，

piāodào wǒ de liǎn shang.
飘到 我 的 脸 上。

Liǎn shang tǎngzhe lèi,
脸 上 淌着 泪，

xiàng nà tiáo wānwān de héshuǐ,
像 那 条 弯弯 的 河水，

wānwān de héshuǐ liú a,
弯弯 的 河水 流 啊，

liújìn wǒ de xīn shang.
流进 我 的 心 上。

Wū……
呜……

Wǒ de xīn chōngmǎn chóuchàng,
我 的 心 充满 惆怅，

bù wèi nà wānwān de yuèliàng,
不 为 那 弯弯 的 月亮，

zhǐ wèi nà jīntiān de cūnzhuāng,
只 为 那 今天 的 村庄，

hái chàngzhe guòqù de gēyáo.
还 唱着 过去 的 歌谣。

Wū……
呜……

Gùxiāng de yuèliàng,
故乡 的 月亮，

nǐ nà wānwān de yōushāng,
你 那 弯弯 的 忧伤，

chuāntòule wǒ de xiōngtáng.
穿透了 我 的 胸膛。

SING SONGS AND LEARN CHINESE

●●● 歌词大意 Main Idea of the Lyrics ●●●

　　这首歌像一幅画，描绘了江南水乡宁静安闲的夜景和乡恋之情。

　　深蓝的夜空，一弯新月；小河缓缓流动；河上有桥，桥下小船，轻轻摇荡，美丽的少女在船上歌唱。歌声飘来，还是那首古老的歌谣，令人不禁感慨：田园生活的确美好，可是又多么希望乡村有新的改变。

This picturesque song describes the tranquil nocturne in the south of the Yangtze River with a mood of nostalgia.

A crescent hangs in the dark blue mid-night sky. The creek is flowing smoothly with a bridge bestriding it, under which a small boat is floating gently. On the boat, there is a beautiful girl singing that ancient ballad. The pastoral life is enchanting, but I wish the village would have some new changes.

1. 弯弯的	wānwān de	crescent
2. 遥远	yáoyuǎn	distant
3. 夜空	yèkōng	night sky
4. 悠悠	yōuyōu	leisurely
5. 阿娇	Ā jiāo	the name of a girl
6. 摇(船)	yáo (chuán)	to row (a boat)
7. 古老	gǔlǎo	ancient
8. 歌谣	gēyáo	ballad
9. 飘	piāo	to float
10. 淌	tǎng	to shed (tears)
11. 惆怅	chóuchàng	melancholy
12. 村庄	cūnzhuāng	village
13. 过去	guòqù	previously
14. 故乡	gùxiāng	homeland
15. 忧伤	yōushāng	sadness
16. 穿	chuān	to pierce through
17. 胸膛	xiōngtáng	chest

 **Grammer Notes**

1. 遥远的夜空，有一个弯弯的月亮。弯弯的月亮下面，是那弯弯的小桥。

> "有"表示存在，前面是时间或地点词语。
>
> "有" indicates the existence, usually with the time nouns or location nouns in front of it.

> 例如：树上有一只喜鹊。
>
> 明天有雨。

> "是"表示存在，主语一般是地点词语。
>
> "是" also indicates the existence, with the location nouns usually being the subject.

> 例如：门前是一条河。
>
> 这里到处都是花草树木。

2. 摇着船／淌着泪

> "动+着+名"表示动作在进行中以及动作产生出的状态。
>
> "Verb+着+Noun" indicates that the action is in process or the state caused by the action.

> 例如：外面下着大雪。
>
> 她穿着一条白色的裙子。

3. 歌声随风飘

"随 (着) +名"意思是"跟随"。这种用法多见于书面。

"随 (着) +Noun" means "to follow" and is usually used in written language.

例如：小李随大家一起走了。

随着经济的发展，人们的生活水平不断提高。

4. 不为那弯弯的月亮

"为"表示原因、目的。可加"了"、"着"。

"为" usually introduces the reason or purpose and can be followed with "了" or "着".

例如：大家都为这件事高兴。

为了找到一份工作，毕业生们作了很多准备。

三个小伙子为着共同的理想组成了一个乐队。

5. 穿透了我的胸膛

"动+透+名"用法中，"透"做动词的结果补语，表示彻底。

In "Verb+透+Noun", "透" is the complement of result of the verb to indicate "completely".

例如：西瓜熟透了。

每次给花浇水都要浇透。

歌手
About the Singer

刘欢（Liu Huan）

1963 年 8 月出生于天津一个教师家庭。1985 年获得北京首届高校英语、法语歌曲比赛两项冠军，进入流行音乐圈。1987 年，演唱《心中的太阳》《少年壮志不言愁》等电视剧主题歌，一举成名。六年后，完成电视剧《北京人在纽约》的所有歌曲及配乐创作，并演唱主题歌《千万次地问》，轰动一时。

刘欢有着超凡的音乐天赋。对别人的作品有超强的演绎能力，自己的音乐创作个性鲜明，流行性与艺术性成功结合。他的嗓音高亢清亮，音色独具魅力，演唱融合多种声乐技巧，充满激情和美感。然而，这位中国内地最成功的歌者竟然是业余的！

刘欢的专业是法国语言文学，现在是对外经济贸易大学的教师，教授《西方音乐史》。更有趣的是，他的音乐完全是自学的。刘欢 19 岁才摸到钢琴，大学四年中，自学了乐器、音乐技术。他一直把做音乐、唱歌当成最大的爱好，并且将文化内涵融入其中。

在近二十年的音乐生涯中，刘欢获得了歌坛几乎所有的荣誉，并被冠以无数美名："中国歌坛标志性人物"、"中国主流歌坛的一面旗帜"、"著名音乐家"、"人民歌手"等等。刘欢真是一个"奇迹"。

代表作：《少年壮志不言愁》《弯弯的月亮》《千万次地问》《好汉歌》《从头再来》等。

Liu Huan, whose parents are teachers, was born in August 1963 in Tianjin. In 1985, he won two champions hips in Beijing's First English and French Singing Competition and entered the musical circle from then on. In 1987, "The Sun in My Heart", "Youth has No Worries" and other theme songs in TV series made him famous all at once. Six years later, he composed all the songs and incidental music in the TV serial. "The Beijingese in New York", and sang the theme song "Ask Time and Time Again of Times", which became a great hit.

Liu Huan has been endowed great musical talents. With extraordinary ability in performing others' works, he has his own distinctive musical style, which combines pop with art. His voice is clear and resounding, and has a tone color with unique charm. His singing introjecting various types of music skills is full of passion and beauty. But this most successful singer is not even professional.

Liu Huan's major is French Literature. Now he is a teacher, teaching Western Music History in UIBE (University of International Business and Economy). What interests us more is that he learnt music all by himself. He began to learn to play piano after he was 19. During his 4 years, college life, he learnt to play some musical instruments and acquired musical skills by himself. He always considers music and singing as his most favorite likings, and endues them with deep literary connotation.

In his nearly 20 years' music career, Liu Huan won almost every prize in musical circle. He is also honored as "a leading man in Chinese singing circle", "a model in the Chinese mainstream singing circle", "a celebrated musician", "peaple's singer" and so on. He is no doubt a miracle in Chinese musical circle.

Representative Songs: "Youth has No Worries", "Crescent Moon", "Ask Time and Time Again", "The Song for Heroes" and "Start Afresh".

作者
About the Writer

　　《弯弯的月亮》照亮了20世纪90年代初的内地流行乐坛，被音乐界公认为中国现时流行歌曲的一首代表作品。曾被港台歌手吕方、巫启贤翻唱出三个版本，还被著名钢琴家刘诗昆改编成钢琴曲。

　　词曲作者李海鹰，1954年生于广州。这是他的成名作。1994年，他作为词曲作家，第一个举办"个人作品演唱会"，名为"弯弯的月亮"。他的作品风格多变，充满美感。

　　很多人以为《弯弯的月亮》里有个可爱的"阿娇"，歌曲背后一定有一个浪漫的故事。事实上，这首歌是词曲作者李海鹰在家一边看电视，一边写，只花了半小时就完成的作品。后来他说，当时脑子里没有任何故事，自己都不知道是怎么写出来的。"阿娇"是广东水上人家对小女孩的通称，并不是特指某一个人。

"Crescent moon" shed light on the musical circle of China's mainland in 1990s. It is considered as a representative work of Chinese contemporary pop songs. It was remodeled by Hong Kong and Taiwanese singer Lü Fang and Wu Qixian into three different versions and was adapted by the famous pianist Liu Shikun for piano music.

The composer and lyricist Li Haiying was born in Guangzhou in 1954. It is this song that made him famous. In 1994, he firstly held an "individual concert" named "Crescent Moon". His musical style is multifarious and full of beauty.

The lovely girl named A Jiao in "Crescent Moon" makes lots of people think that there is a romantic story behind. However, Li spent only half an hour in writing it while he was watching TV. A Jiao is a very common name for a young girl given by boat dwellers in Guangdong Province, representing no specific person.

八《执著》Zhízhuó

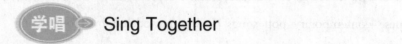

Sing Together

田 震 演唱
许 巍 词曲

1. 每个夜晚来临的时候， 孤独总在我左右。

2. 不管时空怎么 转变、 世界怎么 改 变，

每个黄昏心跳的等 候， 是 我无限的温柔。

你的爱总在我心 间， 你是否明 白？

每次面对你的时候， 不 敢看你的双 眸。

我想超越这平 凡的生活， 注定现在暂 时飘 泊。

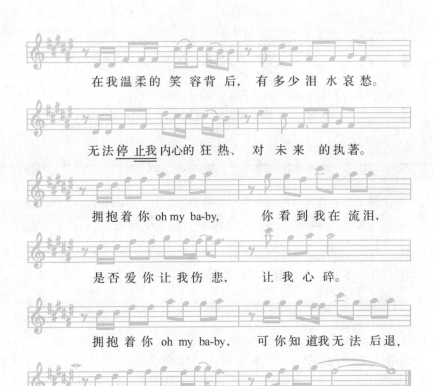

在我温柔的 笑 容背 后， 有多少泪 水哀愁。

无法停 止我内心的 狂热、 对 未来 的执著。

拥抱着你 oh my ba-by, 你看到我在 流泪，

是否爱你让我伤 悲， 让 我 心 碎。

拥抱着你 oh my ba-by, 可你知道我无法 后退，

纵然使我苍 白憔 悴、 伤痕累累。

歌词 Lyrics

Měi ge yèwǎn láilín de shíhou,
每 个 夜晚 来临 的 时候，

gūdú zǒng zài wǒ zuǒyòu.
孤独 总 在 我 左右。

Měi ge huánghūn xīntiào de děnghòu,
每 个 黄昏 心跳 的 等候，

shì wǒ wúxiàn de wēnróu.
是 我 无限 的 温柔。

Měi cì miànduì nǐ de shíhou,
每 次 面对 你 的 时候,

bù gǎn kàn nǐ de shuāng móu.
不 敢 看 你 的 双 眸。

Zài wǒ wēnróu de xiàoróng bèihòu,
在 我 温柔 的 笑容 背后,

yǒu duōshao lèishuǐ āichóu.
有 多少 泪水 哀愁。

Bùguǎn shíkōng zěnme zhuǎnbiàn、
不管 时空 怎么 转变、

shìjiè zěnme gǎibiàn,
世界 怎么 改变,

nǐ de ài zǒng zài wǒ xīnjiān,
你 的 爱 总 在 我 心间,

nǐ shìfǒu míngbai?
你 是否 明白?

Wǒ xiǎng chāoyuè zhè píngfán de shēnghuó,
我 想 超越 这 平凡 的 生活,

zhùdìng xiànzài zànshí piāobó.
注定 现在 暂时 漂泊。

Wúfǎ tíngzhǐ wǒ nèixīn de kuángrè、
无法 停止 我 内心 的 狂热、

duì wèilái de zhízhuó.
对 未来 的 执著。

Yōngbàozhe nǐ oh my baby,
拥抱着 你 oh my baby,

nǐ kàndào wǒ zài liúlèi,
你 看到 我 在 流泪,

shìfǒu ài nǐ ràng wǒ shāngbēi,
是否 爱你 让 我 伤悲,

ràng wǒ xīnsuì.
让 我 心碎。

Yōngbàozhe nǐ oh my baby,
拥抱着 你 oh my baby,

kě nǐ zhīdào wǒ wúfǎ hòutuì,
可 你 知道 我 无法 后退,

zòngrán shǐ wǒ cāngbái qiáocuì、
纵然 使 我 苍白 憔悴、

shānghén lěilěi.
伤痕 累累。

●●● 歌词大意 Main Idea of the Lyrics ●●●

　　这首歌表达的是一种坚定的爱，忧伤、沉重，但又对未来充满希望。

　　夜晚思念时孤独，黄昏约会前心跳，无法面对你的双眼，害怕心中的忧伤流露，用笑容掩盖泪水。时空会变换，我对你的爱不会改变。未来是个未知数，我不停追求，什么也不能阻挡。亲爱的，爱让我心碎，但我不会后退。一定会有那么一天，我不再漂泊，不再平凡。

　　This song describes the persistent love, sad and heavy though, but still filled with hope for the future.

　　In the evening, I feel lonely when I miss you; at dusk, my heart throbs before I date you. I dare not look into your eyes, for fear that my sadness will be revealed, and I try to smile to hide my tears. Time and space will change, but my love for you will not. The future is unpredictable; however, I will continue to pursue my love and nothing could stop me. Love broke my heart, my dear, but I will not draw back. One day there must be an end to my wandering and commonplace life.

1. 执著	zhízhuó	to persist in
2. 黄昏	huánghūn	dusk
3. 心跳	xīntiào	heartthrob
4. 无限	wúxiàn	unlimited
5. 温柔	wēnróu	tender
6. 眸	móu	eye, pupil of the eye
7. 哀愁	āichóu	sad
8. 时空	shíkōng	time and space
9. 转变	zhuǎnbiàn	to change
10. 超越	chāoyuè	to surpass
11. 平凡	píngfán	commonplace
12. 注定	zhùdìng	to be destined
13. 暂时	zànshí	temporary
14. 漂泊	piāobó	to lead a wandering life
15. 狂热	kuángrè	crazy
16. 拥抱	yōngbào	to embrace
17. 伤悲	shāngbēi	sorrow
18. 心碎	xīnsuì	heartbroken
19. 后退	hòutuì	to draw back
20. 纵然	zòngrán	even if
21. 苍白	cāngbái	pale
22. 憔悴	qiáocuì	languish

| 23. 伤痕 | shānghén | scar |
| 24. 累累 | lěilěi | countless |

 歌中句式   **Grammer Notes**

1. 孤独总在我左右

"在+人+左右"意思是"跟某人在一起"。"左右"表示地点范围，相当于"附近"。

"在+人+左右"means "to be with somebody"."左右" indicates the range of the place, similar to "附近".

例如：我生病的时候，她日夜陪伴在我左右。

每当她遇到困难，同学们总是围绕在她左右。

2. 在我温柔的笑容背后

"在……背后"可以用于具体或抽象的事物。

"在……背后"can be used with a concrete object or an abstract object.

例如：李经理站在我背后，吓了我一跳。

他们的婚姻在幸福外表的背后，藏着很多秘密。

3. 不管时空怎么转变……你的爱总在我心间

"不管……(怎么)……总"表示在任何条件下结果都

不会改变，"总"可换成"都"、"也"等。"怎么"表示"任何条件"。

"不管……(怎么)……总" shows that the conclusion or the result will not change under any circumstances. "总" can be substituted for "都", "也", etc. "怎么" indicates "any circumstances".

例如：不管他怎么忙，每天总要陪孩子玩儿一个小时。

不管我怎么说，她都不听。

4. 让我心碎／纵然使我苍白憔悴

"让"、"使"表示"致使"、"容许"时用法相同，都组成兼语句。"让"多用于口语，"使"多用于书面语。

The usage of "让" is the same as that of "使" when both of them mean "to make or to allow". And they are used to form a pivotal sentence. "让" is usually used in spoken language while "使" in written language.

例如：这个消息真让我高兴。

让您久等了！

"健康快车"使许多人重见光明。

怎样使单调的工作更有意思呢？

歌手
About the Singer

田震 (Tian Zhen)

1966 年 5 月生于北京，19 岁开始歌手生涯，靠翻唱港台歌曲起步，后来尝试用自己的声音和方式演唱，名声大振。1988 年，内地歌坛刮起"西北风"（西北民歌风格歌曲），她是这一潮流的代表人物。1995 年凭借《执著》，田震确立了摇滚、民谣、乡村、民族等元素相融合的个性化音乐风格，被称为"内地歌坛天后"。

田震的嗓音富有磁性，演唱风格大气、本色，激情与柔情共存。2000 年，作为颁奖嘉宾出席了第 12 届蒙特卡洛"世界音乐奖"，这是中国流行音乐人第一次走上最高级别的世界音乐舞台。

代表作：《我热恋的故乡》《好大一棵树》《执著》《干杯，朋友》《野花》等。

Tian Zhen was born in Beijing in May 1966. She began her career as a singer when she was 19 years old. In the very beginning, she sang songs from Hong Kong and Taiwan; later she developed her own style and sang in her own voice, which brought her great success. In 1988, the "Northwestern Wind" blowed the musical circle in China's mainland, with Tian as the representative figure. In 1995, with "Persistence" which shows her unique style of integrating rock, ballad, country and folk music, she was honored as "the queen in the musical circle in the mainland".

Tian's voice is magnetic and her singing is grand and natural, full of gentleness as well as enthusiasm. In 2000, as a distinguished guest she attended the 12th Monte Carlo "World Music Reward" ceremony, which is the first time that a Chinese popular singer showed up on the world musical stage of the highest level.

Representative Songs: "My Dearest Homeland", "A Huge Tree", "Persistence", "Cheers, My Friends" and "Wild Flowers".

作者
About the Writer

　　许巍，是一位擅长词曲创作的摇滚歌手。1968 年 7 月生于西安，16 岁开始弹吉他，1986 年获得西安市第一届吉他弹唱大赛二重唱一等奖，从此开始了音乐人生。许巍当了三年文艺兵，之后带着组建摇滚乐队的音乐梦想离开部队，此时写下了他的第一首歌，就是后来的《执著》。

　　这首歌最初叫《亲爱的，别哭》，是许巍写给女朋友的。为了自己的音乐理想，流浪演出、在歌厅驻唱、组建乐队、获得成功、乐队解散……许巍坎坷的音乐人生一路都有亲爱的人支持、陪伴，在他自己都想放弃的时候，这位女友（后来的妻子）鼓励他坚持下去，终于有了成功的今天。

　　1995 年，与许巍签约同一家公司的田震看到这首歌，非常喜欢，把原来的歌名《亲爱的，别哭》改为《执著》，一炮打响。

Xu Wei was born in Xi'An in July 1968. He is a rock singer as well as a composer and lyricist. He started to play guitar when he was sixteen. In 1986, he won the first prize of duet in the first competition of singing while playing guitars in Xi'an and started his music career thereafter. He spent three years in the army as a literary and art worker, and later left there with the dream of building up his own rock band. At that time, he wrote his first song "Persistence", which became well-known afterwards.

The song was written for his girlfriend with the original name "Don't Cry, My Sweetheart". For his dream of music, Xu worked as a street singer first, then a bar singer; later he organized his own band, and enjoyed the success; then the band was broken up... On this rough road he was always accompanied and supported by someone loving him. Whenever he wanted to give up, his girl-friend (wife later) would encourage him to persist in his pursuit of music, which finally brought him great success.

In 1995, Tian Zhen, who was in the same company as Xu Wei was, saw this song and took to it at once. She changed the original name "Don't Cry, My Sweetheart" to "Persistence", which brought a huge hit immediately.

九《同桌的你》
Tóngzhuō de Nǐ

 Sing Together

老 狼 演唱

高晓松 词曲

谁 把 你 的 长发 盘 起? 谁 给 你 做 的 嫁 衣?
谁 看 了 我 给 你 写的 信? 谁 把 它 丢 在 风 里?
谁 把 你 的 长发 盘 起? 谁 给 你 做 的 嫁 衣?

歌词　Lyrics

Míngtiān nǐ shìfǒu huì xiǎngqǐ,
明天　你　是否　会　想起,

zuótiān nǐ xiě de rìjì?
昨天　你　写　的　日记?

Míngtiān nǐ shìfǒu hái diànjì,
明天　你　是否　还　惦记,

céngjīng zuì ài kū de nǐ?
曾经　最　爱　哭　的　你?

Lǎoshīmen dōu yǐ xiǎng bu qǐ,
老师们　都　已　想　不　起,

cāi bu chū wèntí de nǐ.
猜　不　出　问题　的　你。

Wǒ yě shì ǒurán fān xiàngpiàn,
我　也　是　偶然　翻　相片,

cái xiǎngqǐ tóngzhuō de nǐ.
才　想起　同桌　的　你。

Shéi qǔle duō chóu shàn gǎn de nǐ?
谁　娶了　多　愁　善　感　的　你?

Shéi kànle nǐ de rìjì?
谁　看了　你　的　日记?

Shéi bǎ nǐ de chángfà pánqǐ?
谁 把 你 的 长发 盘起?

Shéi gěi nǐ zuò de jiàyī?
谁 给 你 做 的 嫁衣?

Nǐ cóngqián zǒngshi hěn xiǎoxīn,
你 从前 总是 很 小心,

wèn wǒ jiè bàn kuài xiàngpí.
问 我 借 半 块 橡皮。

Nǐ yě céng wúyì zhōng shuōqǐ,
你 也 曾 无意 中 说起,

xǐhuan hé wǒ zài yìqǐ.
喜欢 和 我 在 一起。

Nà shíhou tiān zǒngshi hěn lán,
那 时候 天 总是 很 蓝,

rìzi zǒng guò de tài màn.
日子 总 过 得 太 慢。

Nǐ zǒng shuō bìyè yáoyáo wúqī,
你 总 说 毕业 遥遥 无期,

zhuǎnyǎn jiù gè bèn dōngxī.
转眼 就 各 奔 东西。

Shéi yùdào duō chóu shàn gǎn de nǐ?
谁 遇到 多 愁 善 感 的 你?

Shéi ānwèi ài kū de nǐ?
谁 安慰 爱 哭 的 你?

Shéi kànle wǒ gěi nǐ xiě de xìn?
谁 看了 我 给 你 写 的 信?

Shéi bǎ tā diū zài fēng li?
谁 把 它 丢 在 风 里？

Cóngqián de rìzi dōu yuǎn qù,
从前 的 日子 都 远 去，

wǒ yě jiāng yǒu wǒ de qī.
我 也 将 有 我 的 妻。

Wǒ yě huì gěi tā kàn xiàngpiàn,
我 也 会 给 她 看 相片，

gěi tā jiǎng tóngzhuō de nǐ.
给 她 讲 同桌 的 你。

Shéi qǔle duō chóu shàn gǎn de nǐ?
谁 娶了 多 愁 善 感 的 你？

Shéi ānwèi ài kū de nǐ?
谁 安慰 爱哭 的 你？

Shéi bǎ nǐ de chángfà pánqǐ?
谁 把 你 的 长发 盘起？

Shéi gěi nǐ zuò de jiàyī?
谁 给 你 做 的 嫁衣？

Lā……
啦 ……

●●● 歌词大意 Main Idea of the Lyrics ●●●

　　这首歌轻轻的诉说，把我们带回了学生时代，那些清晰的记忆碎片，那段朦胧的情感经历，都浮现在眼前。

　　同桌的女孩，你现在好吗？我们分别太久，如果不看照片，我都想不起来了。你还留着长发吗？还是那么爱哭吗？记得你跟我借橡皮，我们聊天，说时间过得太慢。你不太爱说话，但你告诉过我，喜欢和我在一起。转眼好多年过去了，你写的日记和我写的信都找不到了吧？真希望你是幸福的，流泪的时候有人安慰。我会记着你，也会把年少时的故事讲给我未来的妻子听。

　　This song takes us back to those days when we were in school and those pieces of fresh memories and misty experience of love appeared before our eyes.

　　How are you, my deskmate girl? We have parted for such a long time. I canldn't have recalled your face if I hadn't seen the photos. Do you still wear your hair long? Are you still so sentimental? I remember that you borrowed my eraser, and we chatted, complaining about time's going so slowly. You were quiet and didn't speak much. However, you told me you liked to be with me. Time flies in an instant. You can't find your diary and my letters now, can you? Hope you are happy, and have someone to comfort you when you are sad. I will miss you. I will tell my future wife about the stories when we were little.

1. 同桌	tóngzhuō	deskmate
2. 是否	shìfǒu	if
3. 惦记	diànjì	to remember with concern
4. 猜	cāi	to guess
5. 偶然	ǒurán	occasionally
6. 翻	fān	to rummage
7. 娶	qǔ	to marry (a woman)
8. 多愁善感	duō chóu shàn gǎn	be sentimental
9. 盘（头发）	pán (tóu fa)	to coiled (the hair)
10. 嫁	jià	to marry (a man)
11. 从前	cóngqián	previously
12. 小心	xiǎoxīn	careful
13. 橡皮	xiàngpí	eraser
14. 无意中	wúyì zhōng	unconsciously
15. 毕业	bìyè	graduation; graduate
16. 遥遥无期	yáoyáo wúqī	in the unforeseeable future
17. 转眼	zhuǎnyǎn	in an instant
18. 各奔东西	gè bèn dōngxī	drift apart
19. 遇（到）	yù (dào)	to meet
20. 安慰	ānwèi	to comfort
21. 丢	diū	to throw

 **Grammer Notes**

1. 想起／盘起／说起

"动+起（+名）"用法中，动词类型不同，"起"的意思就不同。"想起"、"说起"中的"起"表示动作与某事物有关系；"盘起"中的"起"表示物体随动作由下而上。

In "Verb+起 (+Noun)", "起" has different meaning if the type of verb is different. "起" in "想起"、"说起" indicates that there is a relationship between the action and something. And "起" in "盘起" shows that the object is moving with the action upward.

例如：我哥哥来信问起你。
搬起石头砸自己的脚。

2. 爱哭的你

"爱+动／形"用法中，"爱"表示容易发生某种情况。
In "爱+Verb／Adj.", "爱" indicates to be apt to do something.

例如：她特别爱生气。
西安夏天爱下雨。

3. 猜不出问题的你

"动+出（+名）"表示动作完成，兼有从隐蔽到显露、或从无到有的意思。

"Verb+出 (+Noun)" inditates that an action is completed, implying the meaning of from the hidden to the revealed or from having not something to having it.

例如：我看出了他的心事。

到底怎么办，谁也想不出办法。

4. 把你的长发盘起／把它丢在风里

"把"字句在通常情况下都是"把+动+其他"，不能用单个的动词，特别是不用单个单音节动词。

The structure of "把" sentence is usually "把+Verb + other elements". There must be some elements after the verb and monosyllabic verbs cannot be used in this structure.

例如：把书拿着

把房间打扫打扫

把话再说一遍

5. 问我借半块橡皮

"问"在这里是介词，意思是"向"、"跟"。后面的动词多含有"取得"的意思，如"借"、"要"。

"问" here is a preposition, meaning "向"、跟" ("from"). It is usually followed by a verb meaning "to obtain", such as "借"、"要" ("borrow", "ask").

例如：你没问他要一瓶水吗？

昨天，他问我借摩托车，我没借。

歌手
About the Singer

老狼 (Lao Lang)

　　本名王阳，1968 年 12 月生于北京。大学时组织了内地第一支大学生摇滚乐队"青铜器"并担任主唱，在北京各种地下摇滚音乐会与崔健、唐朝、黑豹等乐队同台演出。1993 年辞去电脑工程师的工作，参加《校园民谣1》的录制，演唱《同桌的你》等三首主打歌曲，从此成为校园民谣的代言人。首张个人专辑《恋恋风尘》成为当年中国内地歌手发行量最高的专辑。

　　老狼的声音沙哑但很有魅力。"老狼"这个艺名是因为女友说他唱歌时的吼声像狼叫，给他取的。其实老狼的歌声浪漫温情，歌曲也都柔和温暖。他的演唱风格平淡自然，像是低声自语，又像深情诉说，真诚感人。老狼说自己的歌里没有太深刻的东西，"我只是把我多愁善感的一面表现出来就行了"。

　　代表作：《同桌的你》《睡在我上铺的兄弟》《流浪歌手的情人》《青春无悔》等。

Lao Lang, whose autonym is Wang Yang, was born in Beijing in December 1968. When he was in college, he organized the first undergraduate rock band in China's mainland, and served as the coryphaeus. He once appeared on stage with Cuijian, Tang Chao, and Black Puma on all sorts of underground rock concerts in Beijing. After he quitted his job as a computer engineer in 1993, he joined the recording work of "Campus Ballad One". By his "My Deskmate" and two other hits, he has became the representative of campus ballad since then. His first album "Linger in the Dust" became the best seller in mainland that year.

Lao Lang has a hoarse but charming voice. His girl-friend gave him this stage name, because she thought his singing was just like the howling of a wolf. In fact, Lao Lang's voice is warm and romantic, and his songs are tender and gentle. His singing style is natural and plain as someone's murmuring to himself, also sincere and moving as someone's recounting his feelings and emotion. Lao Lang says there is no profound thought in his songs, "I just try to show my sentimental side."

Representatives songs: "My Deskmate", "Brother in the Upper Bunk", "Lover of the Street Singer", "Un-regretful Youth".

作者
About the Writer

一曲《同桌的你》，朴素悠扬的校园民谣席卷了整个中华大地。演唱者老狼和词曲作者高晓松一夜成名。这首歌获得了 1994 年几乎所有流行音乐奖的最佳金曲、最佳作词、最佳作曲奖。

高晓松，1969 年 11 月生于北京。1991 年从清华大学雷达专业退学。1994 年出版《校园民谣 1》，正式进入音乐圈，这张专辑成为十年来销量最大的原创专辑。他也成为中国校园民谣的领军人物。

这首歌的创作灵感来自高晓松的初恋女友——红。一次，高晓松为她梳理刚洗过的头发，梳完了又盘起，盘起了又放开，突然有了灵感："……谁把你的长发盘起，谁为你做的嫁衣？"几年后，《同桌的你》最终完成，歌声响起，红感动得流泪了。这首歌让高晓松成功了，遗憾的是，他们的爱情却画上了句号。

"My Deskmate", the famous campus ballad, swept the whole China with its simple but beautiful melody, which also made the singer Lao Lang, and the lyricist and composer Gao Xiaoson great successes over night. The song won almost every pop music award in the year of 1994, including "the best song", "the best composer" and "the best lyricist". It was included in "The Review of the Best Songs in the Ten Years", which was published by CRC.

Gao Xiaosong was born in Beijing in November 1969. He dropped off from Tsinghua University, where he majored in Radar in 1991. He had "Campus Ballad One" published in 1994 and stepped into the musical circle. The album turned out to be the best selling original works in those 10 years. Xiaosong also became the leader of the Chinese campus ballad. Later he wrote songs for many singers, which won many music awards. His album "Unregretful Youth" was honored as "the model of Chinese original music".

The creative inspiration of this song was from his first love, Hong. Once Gao Xiaosong combed Hong's hair just washed and then coiled her hair up. When he untied her hair, all of a sudden, he got the inspiration: "Who will coil up your long hair? Who will make you your wedding gown?" Several years later, When he finished this song and sang it to Hong, she was moved to tears. The song made Gao Xiaosong a great success. Unfortunately, their love did not have a happy ending.

十《吻别》Wěnbié

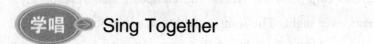

学唱 **Sing Together**

张学友　演唱
何启泓　　词
殷文崎　　曲

1. 前尘往事成云烟，消散　在彼此眼前。
2. 想要给你的思　念，就像　风筝断了线。

就连说过了再见，　也看不见你有些哀怨。
飞不进你的世界，　也温暖不了你的视线。

给我的一切，你不过是在敷衍，
我已经看见一出悲剧正上演，

你笑得越无邪，我就会爱你爱得更狂野。　总在刹那
剧终没有喜悦，我仍然躲在你的梦里面。

间有一些了解，说过的话不可能会实现。　就在一转

眼 发现你的脸，已经陌生 不会 再像 从前。 我 的

世界开始下雪， 冷得 让我无法多 爱一 天， 冷得

连 隐藏的遗憾 都 那么 地 明显。 我和你吻

别 在无人的街， 让 风痴笑我不 能拒绝。 我和你吻

别 在狂乱的夜， 我 的心 等着迎接

伤悲。

Lyrics

Qiánchén wǎngshì chéng yúnyān,
前尘 往事 成 云烟，

xiāosàn zài bǐcǐ yǎnqián.
消散 在 彼此 眼前。

Jiù lián shuōguole zàijiàn,
就 连 说过了 再见，

yě kàn bu jiàn nǐ yǒu xiē āiyuàn.
也 看 不 见 你 有 些 哀怨。

Gěi wǒ de yíqiè, nǐ búguò shì zài fūyǎn.
给 我 的 一切，你 不过 是 在 敷衍。

Nǐ xiào de yuè wúxié,
你 笑 得 越 无邪，

wǒ jiù huì ài nǐ ài de gèng kuángyě.
我 就 会 爱 你 爱 得 更 狂野。

Xiǎng yào gěi nǐ de sīniàn,
想 要 给 你 的 思念，

jiù xiàng fēngzheng duànle xiàn.
就 像 风筝 断了 线。

Fēi bu jìn nǐ de shìjiè,
飞 不 进 你 的 世界，

yě wēnnuǎn bu liǎo nǐ de shìxiàn.
也 温暖 不 了 你 的 视线。

Wǒ yǐjīng kànjiàn yì chū bēijù zhèng shàngyǎn,
我 已经 看见 一 出 悲剧 正 上演，

jùzhōng méiyóu xǐyuè,
剧终 没有 喜悦，

wǒ réngrán duǒ zài nǐ de mèng lǐmian.
我 仍然 躲 在 你 的 梦 里面。

Zǒng zài chànà jiān yǒu yìxiē liǎojiě,
总 在 刹那 间 有 一些 了解，

shuōguo de huà bù kěnéng huì shíxiàn.
说过　的　话　不　可能　会　实现。

Jiù zài yì zhuǎnyǎn fāxiàn nǐ de liǎn,
就　在　一　转眼　发现　你　的　脸,

yǐjīng mòshēng bú huì zài xiàng cóngqián.
已经　陌生　不　会　再　像　从前。

Wǒ de shìjiè kāishǐ xià xuě,
我　的　世界　开始　下　雪,

lěng de ràng wǒ wúfǎ duō ài yì tiān,
冷　得　让　我　无法　多　爱　一　天,

lěng de lián yǐncáng de yíhàn dōu nàme de
冷　得　连　隐藏　的　遗憾　都　那么　的

míngxiǎn.
明显。

Wǒ hé nǐ wěnbié zài wúrén de jiē,
我　和　你　吻别　在　无人　的　街,

ràng fēng chīxiào wǒ bùnéng jùjué.
让　风　痴笑　我　不能　拒绝。

Wǒ hé nǐ wěnbié zài kuángluàn de yè,
我　和　你　吻别　在　狂乱　的　夜,

wǒ de xīn děngzhe yíngjiē shāngbēi.
我　的　心　等着　迎接　伤悲。

● ● ● 歌词大意 Main Idea of the Lyrics ● ● ●

　　这是一首悲伤的情歌，描写情人分手时的无奈与伤感。

　　爱已成往事，说了"再见"，你竟然没有一点儿难过。难道你从没真心对待过我吗？可是你的笑容却让我无法不爱你。我知道，现在我的爱你已经不再需要。一切都变了，诺言不会实现，你的脸也变得不再熟悉。我的心冰冷，却仍然难以拒绝你的吻。我们的爱情就这样以悲剧结束。

　　This is a sad love song describing the sorrow and helplessness of a young man when he breaks up with his lover.

　　Love has become history. You didn't even feel sorry at all when you said "good bye". Is it true that you have never loved me truly? Seeing your smile I cannot help loving you. I know now you do not need my love anymore. Everything has changed and none of the promises will be fulfilled. Suddenly your face becomes unfamiliar to me. My heart is getting cold, but I still cannot refuse your kiss. Our love just ends as a tragedy.

1. 吻别	wěnbié	to kiss good-bye
2. 往事	wǎngshì	past events
3. 消散	xiāosàn	to dissipate
4. 彼此	bǐcǐ	each other
5. 哀怨	āiyuàn	plaintive
6. 敷衍	fūyǎn	to do sth. perfunctorily
7. 无邪	wúxié	naive
8. 狂野	kuángyě	wild, ungoverned
9. 风筝	fēngzheng	kite
10. 视线	shìxiàn	a line of sight
11. 悲剧	bēijù	tragedy
12. 上演	shàngyǎn	to put on show
13. 剧终	jùzhōng	the end (of a film or an opera)
14. 喜悦	xǐyuè	gladness
15. 躲	duǒ	to avoid
16. 刹那	chànà	split second
17. 实现	shíxiàn	to achieve
18. 陌生	mòshēng	strange
19. 隐藏	yǐncáng	to hide
20. 遗憾	yíhàn	to regret
21. 明显	míngxiǎn	obvious

22. 痴笑	chīxiào	to simper
23. 拒绝	jùjué	to refuse
24. 狂乱	kuángluàn	tumultuous
25. 迎接	yíngjiē	to welcome

 歌中句式　**Grammer Notes**

1. 前尘往事成云烟

　　"尘"意思是踪迹、事迹。"前尘",指过去的事情,跟"往事"相同。"云烟"用来比喻事物像云和烟那样容易消失。

　　"尘" means "trace". And "前尘" indicates things in the past, the same as "往事"。"云烟" implies that things disappear as easily as the cloud and smoke.

　　例如:前尘如梦,转眼二十年过去了。
　　　　往事化做云烟,无处找寻。

2. 消散在彼此眼前 / 我和你吻别在无人的街

　　"在"引导的短语表示动作发生的地点,放在动词前。诗歌等特殊情况可以例外。

　　"在" phrase is put before the verb to introduce the phrase indicating the place where an action happens. But there are exceptions in some special circumstances like poems.

例如：中午，我们在学校吃饭。（吃饭在学校 ×）

小朋友们在墙上画了一幅画儿。（画了一幅
画儿在墙上 ×）

3．就连说过了再见，也看不见你有些哀怨 ／ 连隐藏的遗憾都那么地明显

"连……也／都"强调程度深。"连"，有"甚至"的
意思。用"连"引出的事情有两种情况：①说话人认为不
该如此、或可以不如此；②这件事尚且如此，其他的就更
该如此了。

"连……也／都" emphasizes high degree."连" means
"even" and is used to introduce either of the two situations: ①
the speaker thinks that it should not have been like this or it
was possible not to be like this; ② even this matter is like this,
let alone others.

例如：你怎么连我的电话号码也不记得了？（不应
该忘）

今天真热，连不怕热的马马杜都叫热了。
（别的人更觉得热）

4．你不过是在敷衍

"不过"在这里是副词，相当于"仅仅、只是"，表示
限定范围。常见"不过+是+名／动词组"的用法。

Similar to "仅仅" and "只是", "不过" is an adverb here
indicating a limited range. "不过+是+Noun／Verb phrase" is
often used.

例如：别相信他的话，他不过是想利用你。

这不过是我个人的想法。

5. 想要给你的思念

"想"和"要"都表示做某事的意愿。口语里常单独使用，"要"比"想"意愿更强烈一些。也可一起用，多用于书面语。

Both "想" and "要" indicate the willingness to do something. They are often used in spoken language. "要" expresses stronger willingness than "想". They can also be used together in written language.

例如：今天我想去医院。（只是有这个想法）

今天我要去医院。（已经决定了）

他一心想要通过自己的努力买一套房子。

6. 温暖不了你的视线

"动/形+得/不+了 (liǎo)" 表示对情况的变化作出估计。

"Verb/Adj.+得/不+了 (liǎo)" indicates predication of the change of the situation.

例如：饭太多，我吃不了/他饭量大，吃得了。

你说，晒一个小时，衣服干得了干不了？

7. 总在刹那间

"在+时间词+间"表示在某时间范围内。

"在+Time Word+间" indicates the time range.

例如：在五年间，学生数量增加了两倍。

在那一瞬间，我流泪了。

歌手
About the Singer

张学友 (Jacky Cheung)

　　祖籍天津，1961 年 7 月生于香港。1984 年，在一万多人参加的"全港十八区业余歌唱大赛"中夺冠，告别小职员工作，开始了曲折的星路历程。起初，张学友虽然非常努力，但他在歌坛一直没有太大的影响。直到 90 年代，才终于用《祝福》《吻别》等金曲迎来了他的辉煌，名列香港歌坛"四大天王"之首。

　　张学友的实力完全来自天赐的歌喉。他的嗓音浑厚而充满磁性，非常有穿透力，演唱风格深情投入，感人至深。由于擅长演唱各种风格的情歌，创造了无数经典，被称为"华语歌神"。张学友以超人的勤奋赢得无数荣誉。多次在"世界音乐颁奖礼"上获奖："全球最高销量华人歌手奖"、"世界十大流行歌手奖"、"最受欢迎华语艺人奖"……还被评为"世界十大杰出青年""90 年代最杰出歌手"等等。

　　在歌唱事业到达顶峰后，张学友又开始了新的尝试。1997 年制作、主演《雪狼湖》，开创香港音乐剧先河。近年来在全球巡回演出。

　　代表作：《吻别》《想和你去吹吹风》《祝福》《情网》《忘记你我做不到》等。

Jacky Cheung, whose ancestral home is in Tianjin, was born in Hong Kong in July, 1961. In 1984, after winning the first prize in "Amateur Singing Contest in the 18 Districts of Hong Kong", he quit his job as a clerk and stepped on his winding road of being a pop star. He was not given much attention until the 1990s when he welcomed his glorious days after singing "Blessing" and "Goodbye Kiss", which made him the top figure of the "four bigwigs of Hong Kong".

Jacky achieved his fame fully by his gifted voice which is deep, magnetic and penetrating. His true and deep affections in singing make his performances very touching and attractive. Due to his talent in performing various styles of love songs, numerous songs he sang became classics, and he was honored with the title of "God of Chinese Pop Songs". And he has also won a lot of honors including several world music awards, the best seller of music CDs by Chinese singers in the world, one of the top ten pop singers in the world, and the most popular Chinese singer. He was also given the titles of one of the top ten outstanding youth and the most outstanding singer of the 1990s, etc.

When his singing career reaches its peak, Jacky Cheung began new attempts in other fields. In 1997, he produced and acted the leading role in the pioneering musical play "Snow Wolf Lake", which has been performed globally in recent years.

Representative Songs: "Goodbye Kiss", "Wanna Go for a walk with You", "Blessing", "Net of Love", and "How Could I Forget You?".

作者
About the Writer

    90 年代初，香港歌坛兴起国语（普通话）歌曲热，张学友推出国语专辑《吻别》，销量创历史第一，主打歌《吻别》唱遍内地、港台，他也因此成为国语歌坛首席男歌手。

    据说，当时有一位香港歌迷到内地一家卡拉 OK 厅去唱歌，点了《吻别》，却没有这首歌的唱片，他生气地跟服务员吵了起来。老板过来解释，才知道并不是没有，而是点唱的人太多，唱片都损坏了。

    2004 年，"麦克学摇滚" (Michael Learns to Rock) 在中国内地推出全新专辑《让我靠近你的心》(Take Me to Your Heart)。在筹备阶段，他们无意中听到了《吻别》，虽然语言不通，但是张学友的演唱让这首歌特别具有"东方味道"，于是就把它谱写成英文版的《让我靠近你的心》(Take Me to Your Heart)，决定把亚洲最棒的情歌推荐给全世界。《吻别》又一次流行起来。

In the beginning of the 1990s, songs in Mandarin became fashionable in Hong Kong. Cheung had his album of Mandarin version "Goodbye Kiss" published and had the biggest sale till then. As the main piece in this record, "Goodbye Kiss" was sung all over China, and made him the top Mandarin male singer.

It is said that once a fan of Cheung from Hong Kong failed to find this song in a karaoke bar and started to quarrel with the waiters. Then the manager came and explained that as too many people had ordered the song and the disc was broken.

In 2004, the band "Michael Learns to Rock" presented their new album "Take Me to Your Heart" in mainland China. During their preparation, they accidentally heard "Goodbye Kiss" and were attracted by Cheung's performance whice was full of "oriental style". Later they decided to produce the English version of it, "Take Me to Your Heart", to introduce the best love song of Asia to the world and made "Goodbye Kiss" popular again.

十一 《我愿意》 Wǒ Yuànyì

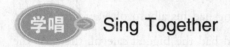

学唱 Sing Together

王菲　演唱
姚谦、黄国伦　词
黄国伦　曲

思念是一种很玄的东西，如影随行。无声又无息，出没在心底，转眼吞没我在寂寞里。我无力抗拒，特别是夜里，噢，想你到无法呼吸，恨不能立即朝你狂奔去，大声地告诉你：噢，愿意为你，我愿意为你，我愿意为你忘记我姓名，就算多一秒停留在你怀里，失去世界也不可

惜。　我愿意为你，　我愿意为你，我愿意

为　你　被放逐天际。　只要你真心　拿爱与

我回应，　(我)　什么都愿意　什么都愿意为

你。

什么都愿意　　什么都愿意

为　你。

Fine

歌词 Lyrics

Sīniàn shì yì zhǒng hěn xuán de dōngxi,
思念　是　一　种　很　玄　的　东西，

rú yǐng suí xíng.
如　影　随　形。

Wú shēng yòu wú xī,
无　声　又　无　息，

chūmò zài xīndǐ,
出没　在　心底，

zhuǎnyǎn tūnmò wǒ zài jìmò li.
转眼　　吞没　我　在　寂寞　里。

Wǒ wúlì kàngjù,
我　无力　抗拒，

tèbié shì yè li, ō,
特别 是 夜里, 噢,

xiǎng nǐ dào wúfǎ hūxī,
想 你 到 无法 呼吸,

hèn bu néng lìjí cháo nǐ kuángbēn qù,
恨 不 能 立即 朝 你 狂奔 去,

dà shēng de gàosu nǐ:
大 声 地 告诉 你:

Ō, yuànyì wèi nǐ,
噢, 愿意 为 你,

wǒ yuànyì wèi nǐ,
我 愿意 为 你,

wǒ yuànyì wèi nǐ wàngjì wǒ xìngmíng,
我 愿意 为 你 忘记 我 姓名,

jiùsuàn duō yì miǎo tíngliú zài nǐ huái li,
就算 多 一 秒 停留 在 你 怀 里,

shīqù shìjiè yě bù kěxī.
失去 世界 也 不 可惜。

Wǒ yuànyì wèi nǐ,
我 愿意 为 你,

wǒ yuànyì wèi nǐ,
我 愿意 为 你,

wǒ yuànyì wèi nǐ bèi fàngzhú tiānjì.
我 愿意 为 你 被 放逐 天际。

Zhǐyào nǐ zhēnxīn ná ài yǔ wǒ huíyìng,
只要 你 真心 拿 爱 与 我 回应,

shénme dōu yuànyì,
什么 都 愿意,

shénme dōu yuànyì wèi nǐ.
什么 都 愿意 为 你。

●●● 歌词大意 Main Idea of the Lyrics ●●●

这首歌描写一个女孩儿思念情人时的心情和她的爱情宣言：愿为爱不顾一切。

相思真是让人难以捉摸，不知不觉占据我的心，无处不在。夜深人静时，独自一人太寂寞。我是多么想念你啊！真想马上告诉你，我有多爱你！为了你，我什么都愿意，只要你也同样真诚地爱我，就算失去一切，我也不在乎。

This song describes the feelings of a girl who misses her lover and her pronouncement of love: She would give up everything for love.

The missing of someone is so mysterious that it occupies my heart imperceptibly. I feel so lonely late at night. How I miss you! I want to tell you now how much I love you! I would do anything for you as long as you love me with the same sincerity. I don't care even if I'll lose everything.

 歌中词语　Vocabuary

1. 愿意	yuànyì	to be willing to
2. 玄	xuán	mysterious
3. 息	xī	breath
4. 出没	chūmò	to haunt
5. 心底	xīndǐ	bottom of the heart
6. 吞没	tūnmò	to swallow
7. 寂寞	jìmò	lonesome
8. 无力	wúlì	powerless
9. 抗拒	kàngjù	to resist
10. 呼吸	hūxī	to breathe
11. 立即	lìjí	immediately
12. 狂奔	kuángbēn	to run wildly
13. 停留	tíngliú	to stop, to stay
14. 可惜	kěxī	to feel pity for
15. 放逐	fàngzhú	to exile
16. 天际	tiānjì	horizon
17. 回应	huíyìng	to respond

1. 如影随形

这是一个成语。"如"，像；"影"，影子；"随"，跟随；"形"，形体。像影子老跟着身体。比喻关系亲密。

It is an idiom. "如" means "alike"; "影", "shadow"; "随", "follow"; "形", "figure". So together it means "it is like the shadow that always follows the body", implying that the relation is close.

2. 无声又无息

"无声无息"是个成语，意思是没有声音。"又"是副词，表示几个情况同时存在。

"无声无息" is an idiom, meaning "no sound". "又" is an adverb, indicating that several situations exist at the same time.

例如：那个女孩美丽又大方。
这几天的天气又闷又热。

3. 吞没我在寂寞里

这句话的正常语序应是：在寂寞里，(思念)把我吞没。

The common order of this sentence should be "在寂寞里，(思念) 把我吞没。"("In loneliness, I was swallowed by the sadness I feel when I miss you.")

4. 想你到无法呼吸

"到"是介词，表示行为、状态所达到的程度。完整的句子应是：(想你)想到无法呼吸(的地步)。

"到" is a preposition, indicating that the action or the state has reached a certain level. The complete sentence should be "(想你)想到无法呼吸(的地步)。"(I miss you so much that I can't breath.)

例如：谁也没想到，事情会发展到这个地步。

这里的温泉热到可以煮熟鸡蛋。

5. 恨不能

"恨不能"也说"恨不得"，表示急切盼望做成某事，多用于实际做不到的事。

"恨不能", which can also be"恨不得", expresses the eagerness to achieve something. It is usually used to refer to things that can not be realized.

例如：我太想家了，恨不能插上翅膀飞回去。

对她，他恨不能把心都掏出来。

6. 就算多一秒停留在你怀里，失去世界也不可惜

"就算……也"用法中，前一分句表示假设让步，后一分句表示对让步后情况的估计。相当于"即使……也"。多用于口语。

In "就算……也", the first clause introduces the presumed concession, while the second predicts the situation resulted from the concession. It is equal to "even if" and is usually used in spoken language.

例如：就算她做错了，你也不应该这样。

就算你不去参加婚礼，也要送个红包啊。

歌手
About the Singer

王菲 (Faye Wong)

1969 年 8 月生于北京。1985 年王菲出版第一张专辑《风从哪里来》(磁带)，全部翻唱邓丽君的歌曲，当时她的声音还十分稚嫩。18 岁定居香港后，王菲以艺名"王靖雯"正式开始歌唱生涯。

1992 年，专辑《Coming Home》中《容易受伤的女人》大放异彩，独特的"灵歌唱腔"让人印象深刻，王菲站到了香港歌坛的顶峰。1994 年改用原名"王菲"，推出国语专辑《迷》等四张专辑，销量惊人，获奖无数，年底举办首次个人演唱会，在整个亚洲引起极大震撼，掀起"王菲热潮"，她终于成为邓丽君之后的"华语歌后"。

王菲的声音非常有特点，音色空灵飘逸、清澈纯净，气息悠长，唱腔技巧高超，擅长运用真假声转换等各种声音技巧，特别是尾音的处理，使演唱自然天成，艺术魅力无限。

她的成就令人瞩目：登上美国《时代》周刊封面，被称为"流行乐歌后"；以最高销量华语流行歌手身份列入吉尼斯世界纪录；被《亚洲新闻》评为建国五十年五十位重要华人之一（唯一的艺人）；被《People》评为全球十大演艺明星之一等等。

代表作：《我愿意》《天空》《棋子》《红豆》《执迷不悔》等。

Faye Wong was born in Beijing in August, 1969. In 1985, Faye Wong's voice was still puerile when she had the first album "Where Does the Wind Come From?"published with all the songs sung by Teresa Teng before. After settled in Hong Kong at 18, she began her career as a singer under the stage name Wang Jingwen.

In 1992, she burst out in radiant splendour with "Fragile Woman" in another album *Coming Home*. Her unique angelic voice swept over Hong Kong and lifted her to superstardom. In 1994, she started to use her original name "Wang Fei", and released another four best-selling albums, such as "Mystery" of Mandarin version, which had won numerous honors and successful sales. In the end of the year she held her first vocal concert and brought a "Wang Fei surge" in Asia. She was then named as "the singing queen of Chinese songs" after Teresa Teng.

Faye Wong's voice is characterized by its pureness, clarity and elegancy. She has acquired extraordinary vocal techniques to produce natural and high-quality singing of lasting artistic charm.

Her achievement is astonishing: she was once appeared on the cover of *Times Magazine*, and was named "the singing queen of pop songs"; she has been listed in the Guinness World Record as the winner of the best seller among Mandarin singers; she was, as the only artist from mainland China, honored as one of the "50 most important Chinese during the 50 years after the founding of People's Republic of China" by *Asian News*; she was also honored as one of "the top ten artists in the world".

Representative Songs: "I'm Willing", "Sky", "Chessman", "Red Bean", "Obduracy".

《我愿意》是王菲首张国语专辑《迷》中的歌曲，在她成为"歌坛天后"的音乐之路上起到了非常重要的作用。这首歌也是曲作者黄国伦生命中最重要的一首歌，让他成为了著名的流行音乐制作人。

黄国伦信奉基督教，《我愿意》其实是为上帝而作的。起初，他的音乐创作一直没有起色，后来他决定把自己的音乐献上，求上帝引导。1994年春天的一个夜晚，为了完成给王菲的作曲，他祈求上帝赐下灵感，结果10分钟写出了这首曲子，从此开始了他的音乐生命和用音乐侍奉上帝的道路。

1999年，黄国伦说服滚石唱片公司成立"基力音乐"，开始将基督教福音音乐推向流行音乐市场。2000年10月，作为第一位华人流行歌手，他应邀在美国纽约卡内基厅演唱了《我愿意》。

"I'm Willing" is included in Faye Wong's first Mandarin album "*Mystery*", which has played imporfant role in her way to "the singing queen of pop songs". Meanwhile, this song has also won the fame for the composer Huang Guolun.

Being a Christian, Huang originally wrote "I'm Willing" to show his love for God. At the beginning, he had a hard time in his music writing. Then at one night in the spring of 1994, he prayed to God to give him the inspiration for composing a song for Faye, and surprisingly finished the song within 10 minutes. Since then he started his music life serving God with his music.

In 1999, Huang Guolun persuaded the Rock Records Company into establishing "G-Power Music" to introduce Christian music into the market. In October, 2000, he was invited to perform "I'm Willing" in the Carnegie Hall in New York, USA. He was the first Chinese pop singer who had ever been invited to perform in this hall.

十二《真心英雄》

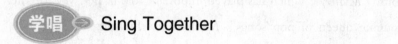
Zhēnxīn Yīngxióng

学唱 Sing Together

成 龙 演唱
李宗盛 词曲

在我心中，曾经有一个梦，要用 歌声让你忘了

所有的痛。 灿烂星空，谁是

真的英雄? 平凡的人们给我 最多感动。

再没有恨，也 没有了 痛，但愿

人间处处都有爱的影 踪。 用 我们的歌，

换你真心笑容， 祝福你的人生从此 与 众不

同。 把握生命里的 每一分

钟，全力 以赴我们 心中的 梦，

不经历 风雨， 怎么见 彩虹？ 没有人能 随随

便便成 功。 把握生 命里每

一次感 动， 和心爱的朋友 热情相 拥，

让真心的话 和 开心的泪， 在

你我的心 里流 动。

歌词 Lyrics

Zài wǒ xīn zhōng,
在 我 心 中，

céngjīng yǒu yí ge mèng,
曾经 有一个 梦，

yào yòng gēshēng ràng nǐ wàngle suǒyǒu
要 用 歌声 让 你 忘了 所有

de tòng.
的 痛。

Cànlàn xīngkōng, shéi shì zhēn de yīngxióng?

灿烂　　星空，谁　是　真　的　英雄？

Píngfán de rénmen gěi wǒ zuì duō gǎndòng.

平凡　的　人们　给　我　最　多　感动。

Zài méiyǒu hèn,

再　没有　恨，

yě méiyǒule tòng,

也　没有了　痛，

dànyuàn rénjiān chùchù dōu yǒu ài de yǐngzōng.

但愿　人间　处处　都　有　爱　的　影踪。

Yòng wǒmen de gē,

用　我们　的　歌，

huàn nǐ zhēnxīn xiàoróng,

换　你　真心　笑容，

zhùfú nǐ de rénshēng cóngcǐ yǔ zhòng bù tóng.

祝福　你　的　人生　从此　与　众　不　同。

Bǎwò shēngmìng li de měi yì fēnzhōng,

把握　生命　里的　每　一　分钟，

quánlì yǐ fù wǒmen xīn zhōng de mèng.

全力　以　赴　我们　心　中　的　梦。

Bù jīnglì fēngyǔ,

不　经历　风雨，

zěnme jiàn cǎihóng?

怎么　见　彩虹？

méiyǒu rén néng suísuíbiànbiàn chénggōng.

没有　人　能　随随便便　成功。

Bǎwò shēngmìng li měi yí cì gǎndòng,

把握 生命 里 每 一 次 感动,

hé xīnài de péngyou rèqíng xiāngyōng.

和 心爱 的 朋友 热情 相拥。

Ràng zhēnxīn de huà hé kāixīn de lèi,

让 真心 的 话 和 开心 的 泪,

zài nǐ wǒ de xīn li liúdòng.

在 你 我 的 心里 流动。

●●● 歌词大意 Main Idea of the Lyrics ●●●

　　这首歌表现了一种积极向上、乐观开朗的人生态度。

　　平凡的人生，有艰难，有困苦，但平凡的人们为了心中的梦想，不断努力，从不后退。遇到困难的时候，朋友们真诚相助，让我们感动落泪。唱起这首歌，忘记所有的忧愁痛苦。人间有爱，有真情动人，每一个平凡的人都是英雄。风雨后，看美丽彩虹，我们共同分享成功的喜悦。

This song expresses a positive, optimistic and vigorous attitude towards life.

The common life is full of hardships; however, the common people continue to work hard to pursue their dreams and never give up. Many times we were moved to tears by the help of friends. Sing this song and forget all the pains and grieves. There is touching love in the world and every ordinary person is a true hero. After the storm we will see a beautiful rainbow, and will share happiness together!

1. 真心	zhēnxīn	sincere
2. 英雄	yīngxióng	hero
3. 灿烂	cànlàn	brilliant
4. 星空	xīngkōng	starry sky
5. 平凡	píngfán	common
6. 感动	gǎndòng	to be moved
7. 但愿	dànyuàn	to wish
8. 人间	rénjiān	the world
9. 影踪	yǐngzōng	trace
10. 与众不同	yǔ zhòng bùtóng	be out of the common
11. 把握	bǎwò	to seize
12. 全力以赴	quánlì yǐ fù	to spare no effort
13. 彩虹	cǎihóng	rainbow
14. 随随便便	suísuíbiànbiàn	free and easy
15. 成功	chénggōng	to succeed
16. 心爱	xīn'ài	beloved
17. 热情	rèqíng	passionately
18. 拥	yōng	to hug
19. 开心	kāixīn	happy
20. 流动	liúdòng	to flow

▶▶ **歌中句式**   **Grammer Notes**

1. 让你忘了所有的痛

　　"痛"原意是疾病、创伤等引起的难受的感觉，可换用为"疼"。

　　"痛" refers the uncomfortable feelings caused by the disease, the wound etc. It can be substituted by "疼".

　　　例如：头痛／疼
　　　　　　肚子痛／疼

　　这里引申为"悲伤"，不能换用为"疼"。

　　Here its meaning is extended to "sadness" and can not be replaced by "疼".

　　　例如：悲痛
　　　　　　痛不欲生

2. 再没有恨

　　"再+没有"用法中，"再"的意思是"另外、又"，常与"除(了)……(以外)"连用。

　　In "再+没有", "再" means "the other, additional" and is usually used with "除(了)……(以外)" ("except..., but...").

　　　例如：除了父亲，他再没有别的亲人。
　　　　　　要上山只有这一条路，除此以外，再没有别的路。

3. 但愿人间处处都有爱的影踪

"处处"是副词，指任何地方。可以用于具体或抽象的处所。"到处"多用于具体的处所。

"处处" is an adverb, meaning anywhere. It refers to a concrete place or an abstract place. "到处" usually refers to a concrete place.

例如：这样的好人好事，在我们那里到处／处处都有。

我处处关心她，可她还是不喜欢我。

工人们身上到处都是泥水。

4. 不经历风雨，怎么见彩虹

"经历"有名词、动词两个词性，在这里是动词。

"经历" can be a noun or a verb. Here it is an verb.

例如：爷爷一生经历了很多事情。

他虽然年轻，但经历很丰富。

5. 和亲爱的朋友热情相拥

"相"是副词，意思是"互相"。常修饰单音节动词。

"相" is an adverb, meaning "each other". And it usually modifies the verb with one syllable.

例如：真心相爱才会幸福。

你把这几个数字相加，得多少？

歌手
About the Singer

成龙 (Jackie Chan)

　　原名陈港生，1954 年 4 月生于香港。在中国戏剧学院（香港）学艺十年，成为武师，开始做电影特技演员。功夫巨星李小龙逝世后，他以"成龙"（意思是"成为李小龙"）的艺名走上银幕。1978 年成龙主演《蛇形刁手》《醉拳》，独创"功夫喜剧"，一举成名。70 年代末到 80 年代，成龙的电影风靡整个亚洲。90 年代凭借《红番区》《超级警察》《尖峰时刻》等征服好莱坞，成为国际巨星。

　　7 岁第一次上银幕，26 岁导演首部电影，至今，成龙拍摄电影近 30 部，一直扮演健康向上的正面角色，宣扬除恶扬善的正义精神。他的电影将滑稽的喜剧和流畅的动作完美地结合在一起，武打特技多变，打斗场景真实，坚持真人表演，将武打融入实实在在的生活。

　　成龙热心公益事业，为了回报社会，1988 年成立了"成龙慈善基金会"，至今已在三十多个国家、五十二座城市做了近百件好事，许多慈善机构和公益活动都请他做代言人，他也因此当选为"2003 年度感动中国人物"。2006 年 5 月，《福布斯》根据好莱坞各明星的善行，评选出"十大慈善之星"，成龙是唯一入选的华人明星。

　　代表作：《醉拳》《警察故事》《红番区》《霹雳火》《我是谁》等。

Jackie Chan, whose original name was Chen Gangsheng, was born in Hong Kong in April, 1954. He studied in the "Chinese Academy of Drama" in Hong Kong for 10 years, and became a martial art master. Later he worked as a stunt man.

After the death of Bruce Lee, he named himself "Chenglong", which means "becoming Li Xiaolong" in Chinese, and began to perform in movies. In 1978, he starred in "Snake in the Eagle's Shadow", "The Drunken Master" in which he created the "martial art comedy" and earned himself big fame. From the end of 1970s to 1980s, Jackie Chan's movies conquered the whole Asia. In the 1990s, with the worldwide release of "Rumble in the Bronx", "Police Story" and "Rush Hour", he became an international star who was recognized by Hollywood.

Jackie Chan first appeared on screen at 7 and directed his own film at 26. So far he has shot nearly 30 films, in all of which he starred a good-natured man, advocating justice and fighting against the evil. His films are all perfect combination of humorous comedy and actions at master-level. With stunts full of changes and real fighting scenes, he successfully blends martial art into real life show.

To return the love of society for him, Chan established "Jackie Chan Charity Fund", and has done almost a hundred charitable deeds in 52 cities of over 30 countries. Lots of charity organizations and public welfare activities invited him to be the representative, and he was honored as one of "the outstanding figures who moved China in 2003". Lately, he was awarded as one of the "Top Ten Charity Stars" selected by Forbes based on the charity conducted by Hollywood stars, and he was the only Chinese star on the list.

Representative Songs: "The Drunken Master", "Police Story", "Rumble in the Bronx", "Rush Hour", "Who am I?".

作者
About the Writer

　　成龙不但是武林高手，而且非常喜欢唱歌。加盟滚石音乐后出版了多张唱片。他说自己只要拍些好电影、唱点儿歌，就会很开心。他唱歌的特点，一个是经常忘记歌词，另一个就是他独特的嗓音。成龙的歌总是给人鼓励，让人奋进，就像这首《真心英雄》，不知鼓励了多少踌躇失意的人。

　　词曲作者李宗盛，1958 年 7 月生于台湾，是台湾流行乐坛最具实力的词曲作家和唱片制作人，享有"音乐教父"和"百万制作人"的美称。《真心英雄》是李宗盛为成龙量身定做的，李宗盛说，他在歌曲的创作上是"男女有别"的，有些大男子主义。写给女孩子的歌一般是温婉的情歌；而对男孩子的期望是向上的、有冲劲的、努力的，所以写出来的歌自然就是励志的、热血沸腾的，《真心英雄》就属于这一类。

Jackie Chan is not only a martial art master, but also likes to sing. He joined the Rock Records Company and released several albums. He said that it was the process of starring good movies and singing songs that made him happy. While singing, he always forgets lyrics. He has a very special voice and his songs always give people encouragement, such as "True Hero" that has encouraged countless people who have lost their confidence and faith in life.

The lyrist, Li Zongsheng, was born in Taiwan in July 1958. As the most powerful composer, lyric writer and producer in Taiwan, he is honored as "the godfather of music" and "milliondollar producer". "True Hero" was specially designed for Jackie Chan. Li said his songs for men are different from those for women. Those for women are always soft love songs; while those for men are strong and inspiring, like "True Hero".

Focus 时代背景（二）

Background Information 2

In 1990s, pop music began to play an important role in people's lives, and the circle of pop songs was thriving and prosperous.

At this time, a new kind of entertainment "karaoke" emerged, and people entered a time of entertainment nationwide. In a karaoke club, anyone could enjoy the experience of being a singing star. The number of such clubs increased so quickly that they almost replaced the once popular singing bars. Since most of the songs were from Hong Kong and Taiwan, the songs of Hong Kong and Taiwan became more and more popular in mainland China.

The radio stations began to broadcast programs of pop music. Since the Music Radio of Zhujiang, Guangzhou came into operation, China had its own talk show program and its hosts for the first time. Before long, Beijing Economic Radio and other radios stations serving the needs of ordinary people emerged. The program of "The Best Pop Song List in Mainland China" was offered on radio and MTV programs were shown on TV. People

进入 90 年代，流行音乐成为人们生活中越来越重要的一个部分，流行歌坛一片繁荣。

随着一种全新的娱乐形式——"卡拉 OK"的登陆，全民娱乐化时代到来了。在卡拉 OK 厅里每个人都可以过一把"歌星"瘾，"卡厅"雨后春笋般出现在街头，几乎取代了红火多年的歌舞厅。夏日的夜晚，连露天冷饮摊儿都飘荡着歌声。由于卡拉 OK 音像带主要是港台作品，因此港台歌曲流行得更快更广。

同时，流行音乐还有了专门的广播电台。广州珠江音乐台开播，中国第一次有了脱口秀节目和主持人。很快，北京经济广播电台等更加平民化的电台也在各地诞生了。电台设立了"内地流行歌曲排行榜"，电视台开设了 MTV 专栏节目。人们每天都感受着流行音乐的蓬勃发展。

另外，"签约"、"包装"成为当时歌坛的新名词。随着内地与港台流行乐交流日益频繁，内地歌坛见识了明星商业化包装的神奇。一批歌手与唱片公司签约，经包装后推出专辑，很快成名。这批由内地音像公司制作推出的新偶像被称为"94 新生代"。内地流行音乐进入了全面签约时代，现代化的明星运作机制开始逐渐成型，原创音乐也兴旺起来。

此时最响亮的声音是"摇滚乐"和"校园民谣"。1990年，六支摇滚乐队在首都体育馆首次举办了摇滚音乐会，引起巨大轰动。在民谣摇滚基础上，出现了重金属摇滚、迷幻摇滚、庞克摇滚等。1994 年，一盒叫做《校园民谣 I》的盒带发行近 60 万张，歌声中无处不在的怀旧情绪与台湾校园民谣非常相似，掀起了内地校园民谣新高潮。

were experiencing the booming of pop music every day.

In addition, some new words such as "signing up contracts" or "packaging", became popular in the singing circle. As there were more and more frequent communication between the circle of pop music in the mainland and those in Hong Kong and Taiwan, people in mainland began to realize the magical effect of packaging. A group of singers signed up contracts with album companies, and after packaging, had their music albums published and quickly got famous. These new idols, packaged by music companies in the mainland, was called "94 Cenozoic". It indicated mainland's pop music was entering into a new "signing up" age. The modern superstar operational mechanism gradually came into shape. The original music became more and more popular.

At that time, the loudest voice was from "rock music" and "campus ballad". In 1990, six rock bands held their rock concerts at the Capital Stadium, which made a considerable stir. Based on ballad rock, metal rock, acid rock and punk rock emerged. In 1994, "Campus Ballads I" was released and sold nearly 600 thousand copies. The nostalgia expressed in these songs was very similar to that in Taiwanese campus ballads. And the campus ballads in the mainland reached its climax.

唱新歌│学汉语
SING SONGS AND
LEARN CHINESE

New Songs in the New Century
新世纪新歌

十三《不见不散》

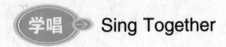

Bú Jiàn Bú Sàn

学唱 ⇒ **Sing Together**

孙 楠 演唱
张和平 词
三 宝 曲

不必烦恼，是你的，想跑也

跑不了。不必徒劳，

不是你的，想得也得不到。这世界，说

大就大，说小就小，就算你我有前世的

约定，也还要用心去寻找。不见不

散。Be there or be square.

不见不散。Be there or be

square.　　　　　　　　　不 见 不　　　　不 见 不

散。　　　　　　　　　　　　　　　　　　　　D.S.

歌词　Lyrics

Búbì　fánnǎo,
不必　　烦恼,

shì nǐ de, xiǎng pǎo yě pǎo bu liǎo.
是 你 的, 想　跑 也 跑 不 了。

Búbì túláo, bú shì nǐ de,
不必　徒劳, 不　是 你 的,

xiǎng dé yě dé bu dào.
想　　得 也 得 不 到。

Zhè shìjiè, shuō dà jiù dà,
这　　世界, 说　大 就 大,

shuō xiǎo jiù xiǎo,
说　　小 就 小,

jiùsuàn nǐ wǒ yǒu qiánshēng de yuēdìng,
就算　你 我 有　前生　的 约定,

yě hái yào yòng xīn qù xúnzhǎo.
也 还 要 用　心 去　寻找。

Bú jiàn bú sàn.
不　见 不　散。

Be there or be square.

●●● 歌词大意 Main Idea of the Lyrics ●●●

　　这首歌表达了一种顺其自然的人生态度。

　　在生活中，我们常常为"得到"或"失去"而烦恼，也总是努力地想"抓住"更多的东西，其实，一切都是冥冥中注定的。顺其自然，耐心等待，平静接受每一个事实。世界真大，我们无法找到对方；世界真小，该相遇的那天我们都不会错过。让我们约定：不见不散。

　　This song describes an attitude towards life which is to follow the natural law.

　　In our everyday life, we are always worrying about our "gains" and "losses", attempting to catch more. However, our destiny is predetermined. Follow the natural law, and accept the reality with a peaceful mind. The world is so big that we can't find each other; and the world is so small that we won't miss each other if we are supposed to meet on that day. Let us make an appointment: be there or be square.

1. 散	sàn	to leave, to disperse
2. 不必	búbì	no need, no need to
3. 烦恼	fánnǎo	worry, to worry
4. 跑	pǎo	to lose, to run
5. 徒劳	túláo	to make a futile effort
6. 得	dé	to obtain
7. 前生	qiánshēng	prelife
8. 约定	yuēdìng	promise
9. 用心	yòng xīn	to make effort
10. 寻找	xúnzhǎo	to seek

▶▶ 歌中句式   Grammer Notes

1. 不见不散

"不……不……"有多种用法，连接意思相对或相关的动词或短语时，表示"如果不……就不……"。

"不……不……" has many usages. When this structure is used to connect verbs or phrases that are related or opposite in meaning, it means "如果不……就不……"(if ...not, will... not).

例如：不去不行

不打不相识

2. 不必烦恼

"不必"是副词，"必须"的否定式，表示不需要。口语里多说"不用"。

"不必" is an adverb, the negative of "必须", meaning "no need"."不用" is usually used in spoken language.

例如：不必再说了，我不想听。

这次考试不难，你不必紧张。

我去吧，你不用去了。

不用给我做饭，我不饿。

3. 想跑也跑不了

"也"表示无论假设是否成立，后果都相同。可以不用连词。这个句子省略了连词"即使"。

"也" shows that the conclusion or result will be the same no matter the assumption comes into existence or not, and the conjunction can be omitted as in this sentence where "即使" is omitted.

例如：（即使）跑最后一名也要坚持跑完。

（就算）你不说我也知道。

4. 说大就大

"就"在假设、因果、条件等复句中，是副词，起承接上文、得出结论的作用。这个句子的完整形式是："（如果）（你）说（它）大，（它）就大"。

"就" is an adverb in a clause of assumption, causative relation or condition. It forms a connecting link befween the above text and the conclusion thereafter. The complete sentence should be "(如果)(你)说(它)大,(它)就大"(if you think that it is big, it will be big.)

例如:只要努力,就能学好汉语。
　　　为了赶时间,就少休息一会儿。

5. 就算你我有前生的约定,也还要用心去寻找

"就算/即使/尽管/虽然……也……",表示动作或状态不因为有某种情况而改变。

The structure"就算/即使/尽管/虽然……也……"indicates that the action or state will not change under any circumstances.

例如:就算我没说,你也应该想到呀。
　　　即使说错,也要练习说。

歌手
About the Singer

孙楠 (Sun Nan)

1969 年 2 月出生在大连一个艺术家庭。中学毕业后做了一名普通工人。后来发现自己很有演唱天赋，于是走上了职业歌手的道路。1992 年，孙楠在印尼连开六场个人演唱会，成为第一个在国外举办个人演唱会的内地流行歌手。此后，作为第一个与境外唱片公司签约的内地歌手，成功地在香港及东南亚发展歌唱事业。

然而，最初内地并没有多少人知道孙楠。1996 年，他用一首《红旗飘飘》正式进军内地歌坛。1998 年底，《不见不散》获得"中国原创歌曲排行榜 1999 年度十大金曲"第一名，奠定了孙楠内地歌坛一线男歌手的地位。随后的几年间，内地几乎所有音乐颁奖典礼的"最佳男歌手"奖杯都被他一人捧走。

孙楠被评价为"继刘欢之后中国最好的嗓音"，甚至被称为"华人第一男声"。他的嗓音高亢，音色纯净，音域宽广，特别是"焰火一般"的高音，华丽优美。演唱风格激情投入，深情动人。

代表作：《不见不散》《你快回来》《为爱说抱歉》《缘分的天空》等。

Sun Nan was born in an artists' family in Dalian. After graduation from high school, he became an ordinary worker. Later he discovered his talent in singing and turned his career to a singer. In 1992, he held six concerts successively in Indonesia, and became the first pop singer from the mainland who held personal concerts in a foreign country. After that, he succeeded in developing his career in Hong Kong and southeastern Asia as the first singer from the mainland who signed contracts with foreign record companies.

However, at the very beginning Sun was known by few people in the mainland. In 1996, he made his debut in mainland's singing circle with "the Chinese Flag Fluttering". At the end of 1998, "Be There or Be Square" won the first prize of the top ten Chinese original songs in 1999, which established his top status in mainland's singing circle. In the following years, he has gained nearly all the awards of the best male singer in the mainland.

Sun Nan is considered as having the best voice in China after Liu Huan. His loud and sonorous voice, his clear timbre and wide diapason, especially his high pitch "as flamboyant as fire", made his singing full of ardour and elegancy.

Representative Songs: "Be There or Be Square", "Please Be Back Soon", "Say Sorry for Love", "The Heaven of Our Love Fate".

作者
About the Writer

《不见不散》是 1999 年同名贺岁影片的主题曲。一个偶然的机会，导演冯小刚听到孙楠的歌声，大为赞叹，并许诺以后一定找机会和孙楠合作。于是《不见不散》就成了两人合作的开端。

这首歌全部采用交响乐队现场录音，音域跨度高达两个八度，极富挑战性。本来是一句大家不经意间就会脱口而出的话——"不见不散!"却被孙楠演唱得如此坚定、执著、宿命，他那充满激情的声音震撼着每一个人的心灵。这部电影也因为这首主题歌而增色许多。

"贺岁片"的创意来自港台电影的"贺岁"概念。内地第一部贺岁片是 1997 年冯小刚导演的《甲方乙方》。这部影片震惊了电影市场，一直被票房收入困扰的内地电影市场终于发现了一种新的电影盈利模式——贺岁片。

《不见不散》是一部轻喜剧。电影讲的是两个到美国去的青年男女，刘元和李清，每次相遇都会碰到意想不到的倒霉事，最后，他们发现自己竟然都离不开对方了……

"Be There or Be Square" is the theme song of the New Year celebration movie with the same title in 1999. The director, Feng Xiaogang, showed great admiration for Sun Nan´s singing when he had a catch of his voice accidentally, and talked with Sun about their possibe cooperation which started with this song.

The span of diapason of this song reaches two octachords, which poses a great challenge for the singer. With the company of a symphony orchestra on site, Sun successfully performed the song with his enthusiastic voice, expressing persistence and firmness with the four simple words 不见不散. The theme song adds much luster to the movie.

The New Year's movies came from the concept of "celebrating the New Year" with movies in Hong Kong and Taiwan. The first one in the mainland is "The Dream Factory" directed by Feng Xiaogang in 1997. This movie shocked the movie industry which had been troubled by the low box-office receipts and brought a new mode of profit making for movies in the mainland.

The movie is a light comedy. A young boy Liu Yuan and a young girl Li Qing get acquainted after they get to the U.S. and experienced unexpected troubles whenever they meet. In the end they find themselves falling in love with each other and cannot be separated.

十四《最美》 Zuì Měi

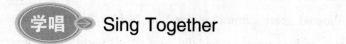
学唱 Sing Together

羽·泉 演唱
羽·泉 词曲

1. Ba—by, 为了 这次 约会, 昨夜 我无法
2. Ba—by, 记得 那次 约会, 那夜 我想你想得

安然入睡。 准备了 十二朵 玫瑰,
无法入睡。 送你的 十二朵 玫瑰,

每一朵都像 你那样 美。 你的美 无
是否还留有 爱的 香味。

声无息, 不知不觉 让我 追随。

Ba—by, 这次动了情, 彷徨失措我不后悔。

你 在我眼中是最美, 每一个

微笑 都 让 我 沉 醉。　　　　　你 的 坏，

你 的 好，　　你 发脾气时 撅起的嘴。 喔 …… 你

在 我 心 中 是 最美，　　　　只 有 相爱的 人 最能 体会。

你 明 了，　　我 明 了， 这种 美妙 的 滋 味。

走 在 街中 人们

都 在 看 我，　　　　羡慕 我的 身旁 有你 依偎。

陷入 爱中的我 不 知 疲 惫，　　为了 伴你 左右

D.S.

与 你 相 随。

歌词 Lyrics

Baby, wèile zhè cì yuēhuì,
Baby, 为了 这 次 约会,

zuó yè wǒ wúfǎ ānrán rùshuì.
昨 夜 我 无法 安然 入睡。

Zhǔnbèile shí'èr duǒ méigui,
准备了 十二 朵 玫瑰,

měi yì duǒ dōu xiàng nǐ nàyàng měi.
每 一 朵 都 像 你 那样 美。

Baby, jìde nà cì yuēhuì,
Baby, 记得 那 次 约会,

nà yè wǒ xiǎng nǐ xiǎng de wúfǎ rùshuì.
那 夜 我 想 你 想 得 无法 入睡。

Sòng nǐ de shí'èr duǒ méigui,
送 你 的 十二 朵 玫瑰,

shìfǒu hái liú yǒu ài de xiāngwèi.
是否 还留 有 爱 的 香味。

Nǐ de měi wú shēng wú xī,
你 的 美 无 声 无 息,

bù zhī bù jué ràng wǒ zhuīsuí.
不 知 不 觉 让 我 追随。

Baby, zhè cì dòngle qíng,
Baby, 这 次 动了 情,

pánghuáng shīcuò wǒ bú hòuhuǐ.
彷徨　　失措　我　不　后悔。

Nǐ zài wǒ yǎn zhōng shì zuì měi,
你　在　我　眼　中　是　最　美,

měi yí ge wēixiào dōu ràng wǒ chénzuì.
每　一　个　微笑　都　让　我　沉醉。

Nǐ de huài, nǐ de hǎo,
你　的　坏, 你　的　好,

nǐ fā píqi shí juēqǐ de zuǐ.
你　发　脾气　时　撅起　的　嘴。

Nǐ zài wǒ xīn zhōng shì zuì měi,
你　在　我　心　中　是　最　美,

zhǐyǒu xiāng'ài de rén zuì néng tǐhuì,
只有　相爱　的　人　最　能　体会,

Nǐ míngliǎo, wǒ míngliǎo,
你　明了, 我　明了,

zhè zhǒng měimiào de zīwèi.
这　种　美妙　的　滋味。

Zǒu zài jiē zhōng rénmen dōu zài kàn wǒ,
走　在　街　中　人们　都　在　看　我,

xiànmù wǒ de shēnpáng yǒu nǐ yīwēi.
羡慕　我　的　身旁　有　你　依偎。

Xiànrù àiqíng zhōng wǒ bù zhī píbèi,
陷入　爱情　中　我　不　知　疲惫,

wèile bàn nǐ zuǒyòu yǔ nǐ xiāngsuí.
为了　伴　你　左右　与　你　相随。

● ● ● **歌词大意** Main Idea of the Lyrics ● ● ●

　　这首歌描写了刚刚坠入爱河时激动、甜蜜的心情。

　　第一次约会，让人心跳，彻夜难眠。玫瑰代表我的爱情，我爱的姑娘像玫瑰一样美丽。人们说，情人眼里出西施，在我眼里，你的一举一动，连发脾气的样子，都是最美的。你无声的美，就这样吸引我，让我沉醉其中，不知疲倦地追随着你。

The song describes the passion and sweet feelings when one just falls in love.

The first date was so exciting, that I cannot fall asleep the whole night. The rose represents my love, and my girl is as beautiful as the rose. It is said that beauty lies in a lover's eyes. In my eyes, every move of yours is beautiful, even when you lose your temper. Your unspeakable beauty attracts me so much that I am intoxicated with it. I'll follow you untiringly.

1. 约会	yuēhuì	date
2. 安然	ānrán	calm
3. 入睡	rùshuì	to fall asleep
4. 准备	zhǔnbèi	to prepare
5. 玫瑰	méigui	rose
6. 留	liú	to remain
7. 香味	xiāngwèi	fragrance
8. 不知不觉	bù zhī bù jué	unconsciously
9. 追随	zhuīsuí	to follow
10. 彷徨	pánghuáng	to hesitate
11. 失措	shīcuò	to lose one's presence of mind
12. 后悔	hòuhuǐ	to regret
13. 沉醉	chénzuì	to become intoxicated
14. 发脾气	fā píqi	to lose one's temper
15. 撅(嘴)	juē(zuǐ)	to pout
16. 明了	míngliǎo	be clear about
17. 美妙	měimiào	wonderful
18. 滋味	zīwèi	taste
19. 羡慕	xiànmù	to admire
20. 依偎	yīwēi	to lean close to
21. 陷入	xiànrù	to sink into

22. 疲惫	píbèi	to tired out
23. 伴	bàn	to accompany

 **Grammer Notes**

1. 为了这次约会

"为了"介绍出动作或行为的目的。组成介词短语放在句首时，修饰整个句子，后面有停顿。

"为了" introduces an action or the purpose of the action. When this preposition phrase is used at the beginning of the sentence, it modifies the whole sentence with a pause after it.

例如：为了照顾生病的父亲，他每天只睡三四个小时。

为了这个理想，我们不断努力。

2. 每一朵都像你那样美

"……像……一样 (这样、那样)+形／动"表示两个事物有较多的共同点。

"……像……一样 (这样、那样)+ Adj.／V." indicates the similarities between two things.

例如：汗水像雨点一样落下来。

他不像你这样聪明。

春天的风像妈妈的手那样温柔。

3. 记得那次约会

　　"记得"强调状态，表示"一直没有忘记"，后面可以跟词语或短句。"记住"强调"记"的动作，表示"不能忘"，后面多跟词语。

　　"记得" emphasizes the state, meaning "having not forgotten". And it can be followed by a phrase or a short sentence. "记住" emphasizes the action of "记", meaning "can not forget". It is usually followed by words or expressions.

　　　　例如：我不记得他。
　　　　　　　记得那是一个冬天的早晨……
　　　　　　　你要记住这个地址。
　　　　　　　小李记住了每一个帮助他的人。

4. 那夜我想你想得无法入睡

　　"得"是助词，连接动词和表示程度、结果的补语。一般的动宾词组加"得"时，要重复动词。

　　"得" is an auxiliary word connecting a verb and its complement of degree or result. In the structure "V + object" with "得", the verb must be reduplicated.

　　　　例如：那个男孩唱歌唱得好听极了。
　　　　　　　小朋友们听故事听得不想回家。

5. 这次动了情

　　"动情"等一些动宾格式的动词能在中间插入其他

成分。

Other elements can be inserted into a verb-object structure such as "动情".

例如：昨天他理了个发。

张先生吃过饭了。

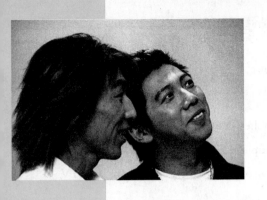

歌手
About the Singer

羽·泉（Yu·Quan）

"羽"——陈羽凡，1975 年 11 月生于北京。因为对流行音乐的喜爱，从 1994 年开始学习创作及演唱，曾为一些歌手和电视剧创作歌曲。

"泉"——胡海泉，1975 年 8 月生于沈阳。十岁开始发表诗歌散文，中学时尝试歌曲创作，1996 年到北京发展音乐事业，也曾为其他歌手创作歌曲并担当制作人。

一个偶然的机会，海泉认识了羽凡，共同的音乐理想让他们走到了一起。1998 年 6 月，他们成立"羽·泉"组合。一年间，成为滚石唱片公司在内地签约的唯一演唱组合，并出版首张专辑《最美》。羽·泉以奇迹般的速度登上内地歌坛，六年中，几乎拿到了所有的"内地最佳组合奖"。

"羽"嗓音高亢浑厚，"泉"则清澈柔和，他们的和声自然和谐，浪漫迷人。特别是在现场演出中，他们声音的魅力和演唱实力，令歌迷"疯狂"。2004 年 5 月"羽·泉"获国际唱片业协会颁发的"超白金销量认证书"，成为内地歌坛"销量之王"。

代表作：《最美》《冷酷到底》《热爱》《没你不行》等。

"Yu", whose full name is Chen Yufan, was born in Beijing in November 1975. As he loved pop music, he began to learn music writing and singing in 1994 and wrote songs for some singers and TV series.

"Quan", whose full name is Hu Haiquan, was born in Shenyang in August 1975. Since 10, he had some poems and essays published, and started to write songs when he was in high school. In 1996, he came to Beijing to continue his music career, and wrote songs for some singers and worked as a producer.

Later on an accidental occasion, the two young men met and worked together for their common love of music. In June 1998, the two set up their own band named "Yu·Quan". Only in one year's time, they became the only band in the mainland who signed contracts with the Rock Record Company, and had their first album "The Most Beautiful Girl" published. Since then their music career developed in an unbelievable speed. They won almost all the best band awards in mainland China in 6 years.

Due to Yu's resounding and thick voice combined perfectly with Quan's clear and tender voice their harmony is natural, melodious, romantic and charming. Especially in their live show, their charm and performance always enchant their fans. In May 2004, Yu· Quan won "the Super Platinum Sales Certification" awarded by IFPI, as a symbol of their becoming the best seller in Mainland singing circle.

Representative Songs: "The Most Beautiful Girl", "Hard-hearted to the End", "Ardent Love", "Can Not Live without You".

　　《最美》是"羽·泉"组合第一张专辑的标题歌曲，是他们自己创作的。旋律轻快、优美，木吉他与优美的和声，歌唱着浪漫美好的青春恋情。这首歌1999年获多个"年度金曲奖"，成为当年 KTV 点唱最多的歌曲，"羽·泉"也因此获得了第一个最佳组合奖。

　　"羽·泉"有着超凡的创作才华。在他们的作品中，羽凡的音乐灵感与海泉的文学功底，达到了完美的结合，风格清新灵动而又激情四溢，每一首歌都是他们对生活、对人生的真实体验，用自己认为最精彩的方式表达着发自心灵深处的声音和感动。"羽·泉"说，好听的音乐不是靠排行榜推荐、唱片公司宣传，更不是去模仿。用心创作、用心歌唱，定会有人用心聆听、用心欣赏。

"The Most Beautiful Girl", which was composed by themselves, is the hit song in Yu·Quan's first album. In light-hearted and beautiful melody and in excellent harmony, they sing the romantic and fascinating love of young people accompanied by wood guitar. This song won many golden song awards in 1999 and became the most popular song in KTV and brought Yu·Quan the first best band award in their music career.

Yu·Quan owns preeminent talent in music writing. In their works, the inspiration of Yufan is perfectly combined with the outstanding literary background of Haiquan. Their music is fresh and filled with passions. Every one of their songs shows their true experience of life. Yu·Quan says the best music does not need media's promotion, or propaganda of the company. It is not simple imitation. Once you compose and sing the songs with your heart, there must be someone who will listen and appreciate them with their hearts.

十五《天路》 Tiān Lù

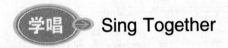

学唱 Sing Together

韩　红　演唱

石顺义　　词

印　青　　曲

1. 清晨　我　站　在　青青的牧　场，
2. 黄昏　我　站　在　高高的山　冈，

看到神鹰　披着那霞　光，
看那铁路　修到我家　乡，

像一片　祥　云飞过蓝　天，
一条条巨　龙翻山越　岭，

为藏家　儿女　带来吉　祥。
为雪域　高原　送来安　康。

那是一条　神奇的天　路, yeah!
那是一条　神奇的天　路, yeah!

把　人间的温暖　送到边　　疆，
带我们走进　人间天　　堂，

从此　山不再高　路不再漫
青稞　酒酥油茶会更加香

长，　各族儿女欢聚一　　堂。
甜，　幸福的歌声传遍四　　方。

歌词　Lyrics

Qīngchén wǒ zhàn zài qīngqīng de mùchǎng,
清晨　我站在青青的牧场，

kàndào shén yīng pīzhe nà xiáguāng,
看到　神鹰披着那霞光，

Xiàng yí piàn xiángyún fēiguo lántiān,
像一片祥云飞过蓝天，

wèi zàng jiā érnǚ dàilái jíxiáng.
为藏家儿女带来吉祥。

Nà shì yì tiáo shénqí de tiān lù,
那是一条神奇的天路，

bǎ rénjiān de wēnnuǎn sòngdào biānjiāng,
把人间的温暖送到边疆，

Cóngcǐ shān bú zài gāo lù bú zài màncháng,
从此山不再高路不再漫长，

gè zú érnǚ huānjù yì táng.

各 族 儿女 欢聚 一 堂。

Huánghūn wǒ zhàn zài gāogāo de shāngāng,

黄昏 我 站 在 高高 的 山冈,

kàn nà tiělù xiūdào wǒ jiāxiāng,

看 那 铁路 修到 我 家乡,

yì tiáo tiáo jùlóng fān shān yuè lǐng,

一 条 条 巨龙 翻 山 越 岭,

wèi xuě yù gāoyuán sònglái ānkāng.

为 雪 域 高原 送来 安康。

Nà shì yì tiáo shénqí de tiān lù,

那 是 一 条 神奇 的 天 路,

dài wǒmen zǒujìn rénjiān tiāntáng,

带 我们 走进 人间 天堂,

qīngkējiǔ sūyóuchá huì gèngjiā xiāngtián,

青稞酒 酥油茶 会 更加 香甜,

xìngfú de gēshēng chuánbiàn sìfāng.

幸福 的 歌声 传遍 四方。

●●● 歌词大意 Main Idea of the Lyrics ●●●

　　这是一首藏族人歌唱新建铁路和新生活的歌曲。

　　清晨的牧场上空，一只雄鹰飞过，它带来了吉祥美好的消息。从远方通往我们藏族人居住的高原，一条铁路正在修建。站在山冈上，看到铁路像巨龙在山岭间飞腾。这条神奇的路，让藏族和其他民族距离更近，我们的生活会更加幸福。

　　This is a song of Tibetans who sing for their happiness in welcoming a new railway and their new lives.

　　In the early morning, an eagle flies in the sky over the pasture. It brings an auspicious message that a railway is being built, which runs from faraway to the plateau where Tibetans live. Standing on the hummock, I can see the railway runs over the mountains just like a great dragon flying upward. This magic railway bringsTibetans closer to people of other ethnic groups, and leads us to a happier life.

1. 青	qīng	green
2. 牧场	mùchǎng	pasture; ranch
3. 鹰	yīng	eagle
4. 披	pī	to wrap around
5. 霞光	xiáguāng	rays of morning or evening sunshine
6. 祥云	xiángyún	propitious clouds
7. 吉祥	jíxiáng	auspicious
8. 神奇	shénqí	miraculous
9. 边疆	biānjiāng	frontier
10. 族	zú	nationality
11. 欢聚一堂	huānjù yì táng	to enjoy a happy get-togethe
12. 山冈	shāngāng	hill
13. 巨龙	jùlóng	huge dragon ·
14. 翻山越岭	fān shān yuè lǐng	to climb over hills
15. 域	yù	region
16. 高原	gāoyuán	plateau
17. 安康	ānkāng	safe and well
18. 天堂	tiāntáng	heaven
19. 青稞	qīngkē	highland barley
20. 酥油	sūyóu	hee
21. 四方	sìfāng	four directions of north, south, west and east

1. 看到神鹰披着那霞光 / 看那铁路修到我家乡

"那"在诗歌中常做衬字，无实际意义。

"那" is usually used in poems to produce the rhyme and has no real meaning.

> 例如：在那遥远的地方，有位好姑娘。
>
> 她那粉红的小脸，好像红太阳。

2. 为藏家儿女带来吉祥

"家"指民族。

"家" means "nationality" here.

> 例如：这是苗家的风俗。
>
> 傣家人非常好客。

"儿女"指广义的儿子和女儿，在文学作品中或某些特定情况下，把国家、家乡等比做"母亲"时，有这样的用法。

"儿女" means sons and daughters in general, and sometimes is used under a certain circumstance when the country or hometown is compared to mother in literary works.

> 例如：祖国的好儿女。
>
> 三秦儿女多英豪。

3. 把人间的温暖送到边疆

当动词有两个宾语时，常使用"把"字句："把+名1+动+名2"。

"把+Noun1+Verb+Noun2" is used when the verb has two objects.

例如：请你把这书给张老师。

大家不要把这件事告诉小赵。

4. 从此，山不再高路不再漫长

"再"与否定词合用时，如果否定词在前，表示动作不重复或不继续下去。

"再" with a negative word before it, indicates that the action is not repeated or does not continue.

例如：她只唱了一首歌，就不再唱了。

他的妻子走了以后没再回来。

5. 幸福的歌声传遍四方

"传遍"是一种短语式动词，由主要动词和表示这个动作结果的形容词或动词构成，动词后的部分作用与补语相似。

"传遍" is a phrasal verb which is formed by the main verb followed by an adjective or another verb indicating the result of the action. The element after the main verb is similar to the complement of result.

例如：孩子长大了。

请你把话说完。

歌手
About the Singer

韩红 (Han Hong)

藏族，1971 年 9 月生于西藏昌都一个艺术之家，藏语名"央金卓玛"，母亲是藏族著名歌唱家。韩红从小热爱音乐，但歌唱之路一直不顺。1997 年，她偶然到中央电视台《半边天》栏目做嘉宾，这期题为《不要为你的相貌发愁》的节目播出后，她的机会来了，命运从此改变。

1998 年推出首张专辑《雪域光芒》，其中的主要歌曲在各流行音乐排行榜上长时间占据榜首，韩红在内地歌坛闪亮登场了。进入 2003 年，她成为最红的女歌手，几乎获得了所有大型音乐颁奖典礼上的"最受欢迎女歌手奖"和"最佳女歌手奖"，终于确定了内地歌坛"天后"地位。

韩红的嗓音高亢嘹亮，音域宽广，音色纯净透明，尤其具有藏族人歌声悠远开阔的特点，被誉为"中国云雀"。她还是一位创作型歌手，曲调的藏族风格、歌词的藏文化内涵，是韩红音乐的独特之处与魅力所在。

代表作：《家乡》《风雨中的美丽》《天亮了》《天路》等。

Han Hong was born in an artist's family in Changdu, Tibet, and was given the Tibetan name "Yang Jin Zhuo Ma". Her mother was a very famous Tibetan folk singer. Han loved music even when she was a little girl but she was not successful at first. In 1997, she was accidentally invited to be a guest at the CCTV program "Half Sky" on the topic of "Do not worry about your appearance", and her fate has been changed thereafter.

In 1998, she released her first album "The Shining Rays over the Snowcapped Plateau" and some songs included in the album were on different best pop song lists for a long time. Han became well-known in the singing circle in the mainland. In 2003, she became the most popular singer, and was awarded "the most popular woman singer" and "the best woman singer" in almost every important prize-giving ceremonies. From then on, her status as the "queen singer" in the singing circle af the mainland has been recognized.

Han Hong's voice is loud and sonorous with a wide diapason. Her tone color is pure and crystal-clear, and has the unique far-flung singing feature of Tibetans. Therefore she was called the "Chinese Skylark". She also writes songs while singing and the Tibetan style of tune and the Tibetan culture in lyrics are the unique features and charm of her music.

Representative Songs: "Homeland", "Beauty in the Wind and Rain", "Day Break", "Sky Road".

作者
About the Writer

2006 年 7 月 1 日，世界上海拔最高、线路最长的高原铁路——青藏铁路正式通车。这趟穿越冰天雪地的列车，是中国人的骄傲。西藏从此告别了没有铁路的历史，实现了几代人的梦想。全国各电视台播出青藏铁路宣传片、纪录片时，都把韩红的这首《天路》作为主题歌或背景音乐。

《天路》的确是专门为青藏铁路谱写的。2001 年春天，两位词曲作者到了青藏铁路施工现场，发现铁路工人和藏族群众都把青藏铁路形象地称为"天路"，就创作了这首歌，送给一位藏族歌手巴桑，《天路》在藏区逐渐流传开来。

2005 年春节前，韩红几次为中央电视台春节联欢晚会送歌，都没有通过。后来听说《天路》的演唱权没有卖出，便立即花 10 万元买下，重新编曲、配器、录音。几天后，这首歌被春晚剧组选中。在春晚演唱后，《天路》火遍了全国。

作为藏族女儿，青藏铁路通车时，韩红应邀参加央视的通车典礼活动，再次演唱了《天路》。

On July 1st, 2006, the longest plateau railway at the highest altitude, Qinghai-Tibet railway was officially open to run. The railway, which the Chinese people are proud of, runs through the land of ice and snow, linking the Tibetan people to the outside world. The dream of several generations has come true. When TV stations broadcast different promoting documentaries about the Qinghai-Tibet railway, they coincidentally chose the song "Road to the Sky" as their theme song or background music.

"Road to the Sky" was specially written for Qinghai-Tibet railway. In the spring of 2001, when the composer and lyricist arrived at the construction site of Qinghai-Tibet railway, they found the construction workers and the Tibetan people calling the railway the "road to the sky". So they created the song with this title and presented it to a Tibetan singer Basang. Thus, the song "Road to the Sky" became popular in the Tibetan area.

Just before the spring festival of 2005, Han Hong sent several of her songs to CCTV's Spring Festival Gala, all of which had been turned down. Later, she paid RMB 100,000 yuan for the copyright of "Road to the Sky", made some revision and did the recording. A few days later, the song was chosen by the CCTV Spring Festival Gala. And just after Han sang it on Spring Festival Gala, the song became popular all over the country.

As a daughter of Tibetan people, Han Hong was invited to sing "Road to the Sky" on the official opening ceremony of Qinghia-Tibetan railway.

十六《浪花一朵朵》

Lànghuā Yì Duǒ Duǒ

学唱 Sing Together

任贤齐 阿牛 演唱
阿牛 词曲

我 要你陪着我,看着那　海龟水中游,　慢慢地爬在沙 滩上,数着

浪花一朵朵。你　不 要害怕,你　不 会 寂寞,

我会一直陪在你的左 右,　让你乐悠 悠。

日子一天一天 过,我们　会慢慢长 大,我　不管你懂不懂我在唱什

么。噢,　我 知道有一 天,啊你　一 定会爱上 我,

因 为我觉得我 真的 很不错。　时光　匆匆匆匆 流 走,也也也不回头,

美女变成老太婆,哎哟 那那那个时候,我我我我也 已经是个糟老 头。啦 啦

啦啦啦啦啦 啦 啦啦啦啦啦 我们一起手牵 手, 啦 啦

啦啦啦啦啦 啦 啦啦啦啦啦 数着浪花 一 朵 朵。

Wǒ yào nǐ péizhe wǒ,
我 要 你 陪着 我,

kànzhe nà hǎiguī shuǐ zhōng yóu,
看着 那 海龟 水 中 游,

mànmàn de pá zài shātān shang,
慢慢 地 爬 在 沙滩 上,

shǔzhe lànghuā yì duǒ duǒ.
数着 浪花 一 朵 朵。

Nǐ bú yào hàipà, nǐ bú huì jìmò,
你 不 要 害怕, 你 不 会 寂寞,

wǒ huì yìzhí péi zài nǐ de zuǒyòu,
我 会 一直 陪 在 你 的 左右,

ràng nǐ lèyōuyōu.
让 你 乐悠悠。

Rìzi yì tiān yì tiān guò,
日子 一 天 一 天 过,

wǒmen huì mànmàn zhǎng dà,

我们 会 慢慢 长 大,

wǒ bùguǎn nǐ dǒng bu dǒng wǒ zài chàng

我 不管 你 懂 不 懂 我 在 唱

shénme.

什么。

Ō, wǒ zhīdao yǒu yì tiān,

噢，我 知道 有 一 天，

Ā nǐ yídìng huì àishang wǒ,

啊你 一定 会 爱上 我，

yīnwèi wǒ juéde wǒ zhēn de hěn búcuò.

因为 我 觉得 我 真 的 很 不错。

Shíguāng cōngcōng cōngcōng liúzǒu,

时光 匆匆 匆匆 流走，

yě yě yě bú huítóu,

也 也 也 不 回头，

měinǚ biànchéng lǎotàipó.

美女 变成 老太婆。

Āiyōu nà nà nà ge shíhou,

哎哟 那 那 那 个 时候，

wǒ wǒ wǒ wǒ yě yě

我 我 我 我 也 也

yǐjīng shì ge zāo lǎotóu.

已经 是 个 糟 老头。

Wǒmen yìqǐ shǒu qiān shǒu,

我们 一起 手 牵 手，

shǔzhe lànghuā yì duǒ duǒ.

数着 浪花 一 朵 朵。

歌词大意 Main Idea of the Lyrics ● ● ●

这是一首轻松快乐的恋歌。

你陪我坐在沙滩上，看着海龟从水里爬上来，我们一起数浪花。什么都别担心，我会永远和你在一起，让你快乐。你说不懂我在唱什么，没关系，总有一天你会爱上优秀的我。当我们变老的时候，还像现在这样，手拉着手数浪花。

This is a light-hearted and happy love song.

You are sitting on the seashore with me, watching the turtles climbing out of the water and counting the waves together. There is nothing to worry about because I will always be with you and make you happy. You say that you don't understand what I am singing. It doesn't matter. Some day in the future, you will fall in love with me. When we are getting old, we will still be hand in hand counting the waves like what we are doing now.

▶▶ 歌中词语　**Vocabuary**

1. 浪花	lànghuā	surf, waves
2. 陪	péi	to accompany
3. 海龟	hǎiguī	turtle
4. 游	yóu	to swim
5. 爬	pá	to creep
6. 沙滩	shātān	sands
7. 数	shǔ	to count
8. 害怕	hàipà	to fear
9. 寂寞	jìmò	loneliness
10. 一直	yìzhí	still
11. 乐悠悠	lèyōuyōu	delightedly
12. 时光	shíguāng	days, time
13. 匆匆	cōngcōng	hurriedly
14. 回头	huítóu	to look back
15. 美女	měinǚ	beautiful girl
16. 老太婆	lǎotàipó	old woman
17. 糟	zāo	poor
18. 老头	lǎotóu	old man
19. 牵(手)	qiān(shǒu)	hand in hand

 **Grammer Notes**

1. 我要① 你陪着我／你不要② 害怕

"要①"是动词，表示请求、要求。

"要①" is a verb, indicating "to want".

例如：你要①我怎么做？
　　　医生要①病人多休息。

"要②"是助动词，表示应该。否定用"不要"，跟"别"可以换用。

"要②" is an auxiliary verb, meaning "should, ought to". The negative form is "不要", which can be replaced by "别".

例如：水果要②洗干净吃。
　　　你不要②这样说。

2. 你不会寂寞／我们会慢慢长大

"会"是助动词，多表示将来的可能性，也可以表示过去的和现在的。

"会" is an auxiliary verb. It is often used to indicate the possibility in the future. It can also be used to indicate the possibility at present or in the past.

例如：明年我一定会来看你。
　　　现在李先生会在家吗？
　　　他怎么会那样做呢？真不敢相信！

3. 我会一直陪在你的左右

"一直+动/形"表示动作持续不断或状态持续不变。"一直"后多用两个以上音节。

"一直+Verb/Adj." indicates that the action or state remains without change. "一直" is usually followed by a disyllabic word or a word with mone than two syllables.

例如：雨一直下个不停。

这几个月我一直很忙。

4. 我不管你懂不懂我在唱什么

"不管A不A"（A是动词或形容词），表示"无论这样或不这样"。

"不管A不A" means "No matter A or not A"; A is a verb or an adjective.

例如：不管来不来，你都打个电话给我。

不管你画得好不好，我都喜欢。

5. 你一定会爱上我

"动+上（+名）"表示动作开始并继续下去，强调的是"开始"。

"Verb+上(+Noun)" indicates that an action begins and will continue, with an emphasis on "starting the action".

例如：听，邻居小伙子又唱上（歌）了。

两个老太太一见面就聊上（天）了。

歌手
About the Singer

任贤齐（Richie Jen）

1966 年 6 月生于台湾一个教师家庭。高中时，英语老师让大家唱英文歌学英语，任贤齐因此对音乐产生了兴趣，开始用吉他弹唱。但他星途坎坷，在音乐圈默默无闻十年后，1996 年底终于以一首《心太软》成名，之后连年获得"最受欢迎男歌手""亚洲之星"等大奖，确立了他的"亚洲新天王"地位。

任贤齐嗓音并不独特，但演唱真情动人，风格清新俏皮又带点儿"苦味"。他的硬汉歌曲、苦情情歌，贴近人们的内心感受，感动着每一个普通人。他的成功不但来自对音乐的执著与不懈努力，还来自他的个人魅力。生活中真实的他与歌中的形象非常接近，因此在娱乐圈里被称做"绝种好男人"、"好好先生"。

2006 年 7 月，中国原创音乐流行榜季选颁奖典礼上，任贤齐获得最高奖"亚太至尊歌手奖"。

代表作：《心太软》《对面的女孩看过来》《浪花一朵朵》《我是一只鱼》《春天花会开》等。

Richie Jen was born into a teachers' family in Taiwan in June, 1966. When he was in high school, his English teacher taught them English by singing English songs, which aroused Richie's interest in music. He began to sing with guitar. However, his road to a star was not smooth at the beginning. After being unknown to the public for 10 years, he finally became popular with "Your Heart is Too Soft" at the end of 1996. In the following years, he gained the prizes of "the most popular man singer", "the star of Asia" and so on, which established his position as "the new heavenly king in Asia".

Richie's voice is not unique, but his singing is touching, with clear and naughty style as well as a taste of bitterness. His hero songs and bitter love songs are close to people's hearts and appeal to common people. His success comes not only from the continuous efforts but also from his personal charm. In real life Richie is very close to the image he created in his songs. Therefore, he was called "the nice man" and "Mr. Please All".

In July, 2006, on the prize-giving ceremony of Chinese original pop music, he won the highest award, "the best singer in Asian-Pacific".

Representative Songs: "You Heart is Too Soft", "The Girl across the Way Look Over Here", "The Waves", "I Am Fish", "The Flower Will Blossom in Spring".

　　《浪花一朵朵》是任贤齐和香港影星郑秀文合作的电影《夏日么么茶》里的歌曲，节奏欢快、可爱，旋律优美。在影片中，任贤齐、阿牛弹着吉他对郑秀文唱，既有喜剧效果，又很深情，为成就一段美丽的爱情起到了决定性作用。这首歌也是任贤齐歌曲中传唱最广的一首。

　　这首歌的作者阿牛是滚石唱片的一名创作型歌手，原名陈庆祥。很早就在马来西亚华语乐坛走红，也出了多张专辑，但跟任贤齐合作《浪花一朵朵》让他走向了更广阔的天地。《对面的女孩看过来》也是他的作品。任贤齐唱红了他的歌，他说小齐是他的"福星"。虽然阿牛已经是一位爸爸，但他依然带着浓浓的孩子气。他的音乐轻松愉快，他说，是女儿给了他很多创作灵感，为他的音乐增添了不少童真的东西。

"The Waves" was sung in the movie "Summer Tea", in which Richie played the hero and the Hong Kong star Zheng Xiuwen as the heroine. The rhythm of this song is cheerful, light-hearted, lovely and the melody is beautiful. In the movie, Richie played this song by guitar and sang together with A'niu to Zheng Xiuwen. The scene is full of comedy and deep affections, presenting a beautiful picture of love in the movie. This is also one of the most popular songs of Richie's.

The writer of this song is A'niu, originally named Chen Qingxiang, a creative singer of the Rock Record Company, who also writes songs. He was popular in the Malay Chinese musical circle and produced a lot of albums. However, this cooperation with Richie in "The Waves" led A'niu to greater success in his career. "The Girl across the Way Look Over Here" is also one of his works. Richie made his songs popular, so A'niu said Richie was his "lucky star". Though A'niu is father now, he still maintains the lovely childishness and his songs are light-hearted and cheerful. He said it was his daughter who gave him endless inspiration and brought much naiveness to his music.

十七 《蜗牛》 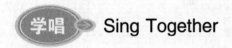 Wōniú

学唱 Sing Together

周杰伦 演唱
周杰伦 词曲

该 不该 搁下 重重 的 壳, 寻 找 到底 哪里有 蓝

天? 随 着 轻 轻的 风 轻 轻 地 飘, 历

经 的 伤都 不感觉 疼。 我

要 一步一步往上 爬, 等待 阳 光 静静 看着 它的

脸。 小 小的 天 有 大 大 的 梦 想, 重 重 的

壳 裹着 轻轻 的 仰 望。 我 要 一步一步往上

爬, 在 最高 点 乘着 叶片 往 前 飞, 小 小 的
任 风 吹

天　　流过的泪和　汗，　　　总有一天　我有属于我的
干　　流过的泪和　汗，

天。　　　　　我　天　我有属于　　我　的天。

歌词 Lyrics

Gāi bu gāi gēxià zhòngzhòng de ké,
该　不　该　搁下　　重重　　的　壳，

xúnzhǎo dàodǐ nǎli yǒu lántiān?
寻找　　到底　哪里　有　　蓝天？

Suízhe qīngqīng de fēng qīngqīng de piāo,
随着　　轻轻　的　风　轻轻　地　飘，

lìjīng de shāng dōu bù gǎnjué téng.
历经　的　伤　都　不　感觉　　疼。

Wǒ yào yí bù yí bù wǎng shàng pá,
我　要　一步　一步　往　　上　爬，

děngdài yángguāng jìngjìng kànzhe tā de liǎn,
等待　　阳光　　静静　看着　它　的　脸，

xiǎoxiǎo de tiān yǒu dàdà de mèngxiǎng,
小小　的　天　有　大大　的　梦想，

zhòngzhòng de ké guǒzhe qīngqīng de yǎngwàng.
重重　　的　壳　裹着　轻轻　的　仰望。

Wǒ yào yí bù yí bù wǎng shàng pá,
我 要 一 步 一 步 往 上 爬,
zài zuì gāo diǎn chéngzhe yèpiàn wǎng
在 最 高 点 乘着 叶片 往
qián fēi,
前 飞,
xiǎoxiǎo de tiān liúguo de lèi hé hàn,
小小 的 天 流过 的 泪 和 汗,
rèn fēng chuīgān liúguo de lèi hé hàn,
(任 风 吹干 流过 的 泪 和 汗,)
zǒng yǒu yì tiān wǒ yǒu shǔyú wǒ de tiān.
总 有 一 天 我 有 属于 我 的 天。

●●● 歌词大意 Main Idea of the Lyrics ●●●

　　这首歌描写一只蜗牛为了梦想不断努力的情景。

　　我是一只小小的蜗牛，背着重重的壳，努力地向上爬，想找到属于自己的一片天空。每一步都是那么艰难，流着泪、流着汗，不知受过多少次伤。风轻轻吹过来，所有痛苦都没有了，因为风可以让我飞。阳光静静洒下来，向上望一望，那片天空有我的梦。我相信，只要努力，总有一天，我的梦想会实现。

　　The song describes the scene that a little snail is climbing hard towards its goal.

　　I am a little snail with a heavy shell on my back. I am climbing hard upward in search of a piece of sky belonging to me. I take each step with hardship, tears and sweat, and I have had a lot of wounds. The gentle breeze swept all my pains away, for it can help me fly. In the tranquil shedding of sunshine, I look up into the sky where there is my dream. I believe that my perseverance and hard work will make my dream come true one day.

1. 蜗牛	wōniú	snail
2. 该	gāi	should
3. 搁	gē	to put
4. 壳	ké	shell
5. 寻找	xúnzhǎo	to look for
6. 到底	dàodǐ	on earth
7. 蓝天	lántiān	sky
8. 飘	piāo	to float
9. 历经	lìjīng	to experience
10. 伤	shāng	wound, injury
11. 感觉	gǎnjué	to feel
12. 爬	pá	to climb
13. 静	jìng	quiet
14. 梦想	mèngxiǎng	dream
15. 裹	guǒ	to wrap
16. 仰望	yǎngwàng	to look up
17. 乘	chéng	to ride
18. 叶片	yèpiàn	leaf
19. 任	rèn	to allow, to let
20. 属于	shǔyú	to belong to

 **Grammer Notes**

1. 该不该搁下重重的壳

　　"该"是助动词，修饰谓语，表示理应如此，应该。否定式是"不该"。

　　"该" is an auxiliary verb modifying the verb predicate, indicating that it should be this way. Its negative form is "不该".

　　　例如：我该走了。
　　　　　　你不该一个人去。

　　"该不该"是"动+不／没+动"的句式，表示疑问。

　　The struchane of "该不该" is "Verb+不／没+Verb", used to question something.

　　　例如：我该不该去？
　　　　　　你想想，你该不该这样？

2. 寻找到底哪里有蓝天

　　"到底"是副词，用于疑问句时，表示追究事物的真相。用在动词、形容词或主语前。不能用于带"吗"的问句。

　　"到底" is an adverb used in an interrogative sentence to further question something. It is used before a verb, adjective or subject, and can not be used in an interrogative question with "吗".

例如：他到底是谁？

雨到底大不大？

到底谁错了？

3. 随着 / 看着 / 裹着 / 乘着

"着"是助词，表示动作正在进行或状态正在持续。"动 / 形+着"结构中不能加入任何成分，且动词多为单音节。

"着" is an auxiliary verb indicating that an action is proceeding or a state continues. No other elements can be inserted into "Verb / Adj.+着". The verb is always a monosyllabic one.

例如：我等着刘小姐打电话给我。

最近，他一直忙着工作，很少关心妻子。

4. 往上爬 / 往前飞

"往"是介词，表示动作的方向。跟表示方位、地点的词组合，用在动词前。

"往" is a preposition indicating the direction of an action. It is used before a verb together with a direction or location noun.

例如：请你往门外看。

人往高处走，水往低处流。

5. 总有一天我有属于我的天

"总"是副词，表示推测、估计。

"总" is an adverb indicating assumption or estimation.

例如：这个城市总有三百年的历史吧？

妹妹比你小，总不会是她打你吧？

周杰伦 (Jay Chou)

1979 年 1 月生于台湾一个教师家庭,从小学习音乐。一次,别人帮他报名参加歌唱比赛,他不敢独唱,就为朋友钢琴伴奏。后来由于创作的曲谱非常出色,得到一份专职写歌的工作。2000 年作为歌手推出首张专辑《Jay 周杰伦》,大获成功,成为"台湾本土 R&B 小天王",被称为"音乐才子",随后几年红遍亚洲。

周杰伦的演唱最大特点是"吐字不清",被很多人批评,但这正是他音乐魅力的一部分。他的声音与节奏、旋律共同构成"周杰伦式"音乐,另类、独特,极具吸引力。他的创作吸收了各类型音乐的精华,充满幻想与活力。同时,周杰伦还为许多歌手量身定做歌曲,风格各异,显示出他超强的词曲创作能力。

从默默无闻的写歌人,到亚洲最受欢迎的流行歌手,周杰伦获得无数荣誉,甚至被评价为"E 世代不朽的音乐先锋",成为这个时代流行文化的符号,周杰伦用音乐传达着这一代人的精神和情绪。

代表作:《双截棍》《爱在西元前》《半岛铁盒》《东风破》《七里香》等。

Jay was born in a teachers' family in Taiwan and had studied music since his childhood. Once someone put his name down for a singing contest. As he dared not to sing solo, he played accompany on piano for his friend. Later, due to his perfect scoring skill, he got a full time job as a song writer. In 2000, he as a singer had his first album "Jay" published, which brought great success to him and made him "the little king of R&B in Taiwan" and "the talented man of music". In the following years, he has been very popular in Asia.

Jay's most obvious and widely criticized characteristic in singing is his unclear pronunciation. However, this is just where his charm lies. His voice, melody and rhythm together make the unique music of his style, which is distinguishing and attractive. He absorbed and integrated the quintessence of various kinds of music into his own. Meanwhile, he produces songs for other singers according to their own specific characteristics, which shows his extraordinary ability in music creation.

From an unknown song writer to the most popular pop singer in Asia, Zhou has gained countless prizes and even been recognized as "the everlasting musical pioneer in E era" and an icon of popular culture of contemporary age. Jay conveys the spirits and feelings of this generation with his music.

Representative Songs: "Nunchakus", "Love before Christ", "Iron Box of an Island", "Lute", "Daphane".

《蜗牛》是周杰伦为女歌手许茹芸写的。不是 R&B 风格。

周杰伦创作《蜗牛》时正是事业低潮期。那时他还没有做歌手，整天帮人写歌，心情非常不好，于是决定写一首歌勉励一下自己，希望现在的年轻人能够像蜗牛一样，为了自己的目标一步一步往前爬。

2001 年，《蜗牛》被选入了上海初中一年级《音乐》教材。2005 年 3 月，由于思想内容好，也容易唱，被收入"上海市中学生爱国主义歌曲推荐目录"，同时被收入的还有《真心英雄》《中国人》等多首港台流行歌曲。这是内地第一次由政府选择青少年喜欢的歌曲向他们推荐。借着周杰伦的偶像号召力，希望《蜗牛》积极向上的思想对青少年会有好的影响。

"Snail" is a song written by Jay for Xu Ruyun, but not in the R&B style.

When Jay was composing this song, his career was at a low ebb. At that time, he was not a singer yet and was writing songs for others all day. Zhou was in a bad mood. He decided to write a song with the hope that it could encourage himself and the youth today to struggle for the goals step by step, just like the snail does.

In 2001, "Snail" was selected in a music textbook for middle school students in Shanghai. In March, 2005, due to the inspiring theme and easy-learnt rhythm, this song was included in the "patriotic songs for Shanghai middle school students". Popular songs such as "True Hero" and "Chinese" from Hong Kong and Taiwan were also selected in the list. This was the first time that the government in the mainland recommended the popular songs that young students like. By virtue of Jay's influence, the government hopes the spirit of "Snail" would produce positive effects on teenagers.

十八《挥着翅膀的女孩》

Huīzhe Chìbǎng de Nǚhái

学唱 Sing Together

容祖儿　演唱
黄伟文　词
陈光荣　曲

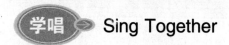

1. 当我还是一个　懵懂的女孩, 遇到　爱, 不懂爱, 从过
2. 我已不是那个　懵懂的女孩, 遇到　爱, 用力爱, 　仍

去　到现在。直到他也离开, 留我　在云海徘徊, 明白
信　真爱。风雨来不避开, 谦虚　把头低下来, 像沙

没人能取代他曾　给我的信　赖。See me fly, 　I'm proud to fly up
鸥来去天地只为　寻一个奇　迹。See me fly, 　I'm proud to fly up

high. 不能一直依　赖, 别人给我拥　戴。 Believe me I can
high. 生命已经打　开, 我要那种精　彩。 Believe me I can

fly,　I'm singing　in the sky.　就算风雨覆　盖，　我也不怕重
fly,　I'm singing　in the sky.　你曾经对我　说，　做勇敢的女

来。　　　　孩。　　我盼有　一天能和

你相见，　骄傲地　对着天空说，　是　借着你的风。Let me

D.S.

孩。　　我不会孤　单，　因　为你

渐慢

都　在。

歌词 Lyrics

Dāng wǒ hái shì yí ge měngdǒng de nǚhái,
当　我　还　是　一个　懵懂　的　女孩，

yùdào ài, bù dǒng ài,
遇到　爱，不　懂　爱，

cóng guòqù dào xiànzài.
从　过去　到　现在。

Zhídào tā yě líkāi,
直到　他　也　离开，

liú wǒ zài yúnhǎi páihuái,
留 我 在 云海 徘徊,

míngbai méi rén néng qǔdài
明白 没 人 能 取代

tā céng gěi wǒ de xìnlài.
他 曾 给 我 的 信赖。

See me fly, I'm proud to fly up high.

Bù néng yìzhí yīlài, biéren gěi wǒ yōngdài.
不 能 一直 依赖,别人 给 我 拥戴。

Believe me I can fly, I'm singing in the sky.

Jiùsuàn fēngyǔ fùgài,
就算 风雨 覆盖,

wǒ yě bú pà chóng lái
我 也 不 怕 重 来。

Wǒ yǐ bú shì nàge měngdǒng de nǚhái,
我 已 不 是 那个 懵懂 的 女孩,

yùdào ài, yònglì ài,
遇到 爱,用力 爱,

réng xìn zhēn ài.
仍 信 真 爱。

fēngyǔ lái bú bìkāi,
风雨 来 不 避开,

qiānxū bǎ tóu dī xiàlái,
谦虚 把 头 低 下来,

xiàng shā'ōu lái qù tiāndì,
像 沙鸥 来 去 天地,

zhǐ wèi xún yí ge qíjī.
只 为 寻 一 个 奇迹。

See me fly, I'm proud to fly up high.

Shēngmìng yǐjīng dǎkāi,
生命 已经 打开,

wǒ yào nà zhǒng jīngcǎi.
我 要 那 种 精彩。

Believe me I can fly, I'm singing in the sky.

Nǐ céngjīng duì wǒ shuō,
你 曾经 对 我 说,

zuò yǒnggǎn de nǚhái.
做 勇敢 的 女孩。

Wǒ pàn yǒu yì tiān néng hé nǐ xiāngjiàn,
我 盼 有一 天 能 和 你 相见,

jiāo'ào de duìzhe tiānkōng shuō,
骄傲 地 对着 天空 说,

shì jièzhe nǐ de fēng.
是 借着 你 的 风。

Let me fly, I'm proud to fly up high.

Shēngmìng yǐjīng dǎkāi,
生命 已经 打开,

wǒ yào nà zhǒng jīngcǎi.
我 要 那 种 精彩。

Believe me I can fly, I'm singing in the sky.

Nǐ céngjīng duì wǒ shuō,
你 曾经 对 我 说,

zuò yǒnggǎn de nǚhái.
做 勇敢 的 女孩。

Wǒ bú huì gūdān, yīnwèi nǐ dōu zài.
我 不 会 孤单, 因为 你 都 在。

●●● 歌词大意 Main Idea of the Lyrics ●●●

　　这首歌描写了一个女孩的成长感受。

　　曾经是一个不懂怎样去爱的小女孩，当那个可以依靠的人离去，没有人呵护，小女孩终于长大了，像沙鸥在风雨中展翅。遇到困难，低下头迎风而上，在高高的天空中骄傲地飞翔。勇敢的女孩，相信真爱，也懂得去爱，找到了人生的精彩。

　　The song describes the feelings of a girl when she is growing up.

　　This little girl, who once did not know how to love, could not get any care when the person she depended on left. She has finally grown up, like a sea mew flying in the storm. When in troubles and difficulties, she lowers her head, struggles against the wind and flies in the sky proudly. The brave girl believing true love now understands how to love and has found the wonder of life.

1. 挥	huī	to fly
2. 翅膀	chìbǎng	wing
3. 懵懂	měngdǒng	ignorant
4. 留	liú	to leave
5. 云海	yúnhǎi	a sea of clouds
6. 徘徊	páihuái	to walk back and forth, to linger
7. 取代	qǔdài	to replace
8. 信赖	xìnlài	to trust
9. 依赖	yīlài	to depend on
10. 拥戴	yōngdài	to support, to favor
11. 覆盖	fùgài	to cover with
12. 重	chóng	(start) again
13. 仍	réng	still
14. 避	bì	to shun
15. 谦虚	qiānxū	modest
16. 沙鸥	shā'ōu	seagull
17. 奇迹	qíjì	miracle
18. 精彩	jīngcǎi	magnificance
19. 勇敢	yǒnggǎn	brave
20. 盼	pàn	to expect
21. 骄傲	jiāo'ào	proud

 **Grammer Notes**

1. 直到他也离开

　　"直到"表示动作或状态在某一段时间、空间或范围内是持续发生或存在的。

　　"直" is used together with "到" to indicate that an action goes on during a period of time, or a state remains in certain space or time range.

> 例如：这里直到50年代，才有了公共汽车。(时间)
>
> 儿子看着父亲的背影，直到他走远、看不见了。(空间)
>
> 参加比赛的，从八岁直到八十岁，各个年龄段的都有。(范围)

2. 我也不怕重来

　　"来"表示做某个动作，代替意义具体的动词。

　　"来" is used to substitute a verb of concrete action.

> 例如：唱得好！再来一个！(=再唱一个)
>
> 大家别客气，自己来！(=自己夹菜)

3. 风雨来不避开

　　"动+开(+名)"表示人或事物随动作离开。"开"是趋向动词。

"Verb + 开 (+ Noun)" indicates that a person or object leaves with an action. "开" is a directional verb.

例如：工作太忙，我走不开。

你不喜欢他，就躲开他嘛。

4. 骄傲地对着天空说

"对"在这里是动词，表示"面对、朝、向"。常带"着"或其他成分。

Here "对" is a verb meaning "facing", "towards" and is usually followed by "着" or other elements.

例如：我家的窗户对着马路。

背对着人不礼貌。

5. 是借着你的风

"借"在这里是"凭借、利用"的意思。常与"着"连用。

"借" means "make use of" here and is usually followed by "着".

例如：我想借着这个机会，跟他谈谈。

他借着去卫生间，走了。

歌手
About the Singer

容祖儿 (Joey Yung)

　　1980年6月生于香港，从小就立志做歌星。15岁时，拿了五个歌唱比赛的冠军，进入歌坛。1999年首张专辑《未知》获香港唱片销售榜第一名，并创纪录，在榜上停留23周。

　　2003年以一首《我的骄傲》获得"全球华人至尊金曲"、"全年最高销量女歌手"、"最受欢迎女歌手"等大奖，成为香港歌坛新一代"天后"。2005年在港台、内地各大音乐颁奖典礼上大获丰收，特别是香港十大中文金曲颁奖盛典中，一举夺得"最优秀女歌手"等五项大奖，是获奖最多的歌手。

　　容祖儿的嗓音清纯甜美、温柔可爱，唱功出色，属于实力派歌手。她也自嘲自己是因为长得不够美丽，所以才走实力派路线。如今，她在音乐、影视、广告等方面发展成功，事业如日中天。

　　代表作:《挥着翅膀的女孩》《不容错失》《谁来爱我》《独照》等。

Joey Yung, born in Hong Kong in June 1980, made up her mind to be a singing star in her childhood. When she was 15 years old, she won five championships in singing competitions and began her singing career. Her first album "Unknown" topped the best sellers of records in Hong Kong in 1999 and broke the record by remaining at the top in the list for 23 weeks.

The song "My Pride" brought her prizes of "the best Chinese song in the world", "the best seller by female vocalist" and "the most popular woman singer", and was recognized as the "queen" of the new generation in the singing circle in Hong Kong. In 2005, she won many prizes at musical award ceremonies in Hong Kong, Taiwan and the mainland, especially the award ceremony of Hong Kong Top Ten Chinese Golden Songs, where she won five awards including "the best female singer".

Joey's voice is pure, sweet and lovely. She is a competent singer who has achieved her success through hard work. She once joked that as she was not beautiful enough she had to depend on her ability. Now she is succeeful in music, movie and ads, reaching the summit of her career.

Representative Songs: "The Girl Flying With Wings", "Don't Miss It", "Who Loves Me", "Photo Alone".

作者
About the Writer

这首歌有三个版本，英语版《Proud of You》、粤语版《我的骄傲》、国语（普通话）版《挥着翅膀的女孩》。

这首歌最初是一家地产公司的广告歌，名字叫做《Proud of You》，是一首短小的英文歌。播出之后商家感觉还不错，就想把广告做大，让曲作者陈光荣把曲子写完整，再找词作者黄伟文填上广东话歌词，这就是《我的骄傲》。之后，广告商通过民意调查，从众多歌手中选择容祖儿演唱。后来容祖儿进军国语市场，又将歌曲填上了普通话歌词，就成了《挥着翅膀的女孩》。

2005年，容祖儿在中央电视台春节联欢晚会的舞台上，身穿白裙，展开雪白的"翅膀"，坐在空中的秋千上，再次演唱了这首当时已红遍内地的歌，这首歌也就成了她最广为人知的作品。

This song has three versions, the English one "Proud of You", the Cantonese one "My Proud" and the Mandarin one "The Girl with Wings".

This song was originally a small piece of English song with the title "Proud of You", sung in an advertisement for an estate company, who later decided to perfect it. They then asked the composer Chen Guangrong and lyric writer Huang Weiwen to complete the song and use Cantonese to replace the English lyrics, which gave birth to the Cantonese version "My Proud". Then, through a mass survey, Joey Yung was selected from many singers to perform this song. After she started to step into the mainland market, the Mandarin version of the song titled "The Girl with Wings" was born.

In 2005, on the CCTV Spring Festival Gala, Joey, dressed like an angel and sitting on a sky-high swing, sang this popular song. It has also become the most widely known song of hers.

SING SONGS AND LEARN CHINESE

Focus 时代背景（三）
Background Information 3

Entering into the 21st Century, the communication between domestic and aboard musical circles becomes more convenient. People's taste becomes diversified: R&B, Korean Flow, Punk, Pop and Rock, etc. More and more new singers have emerged, many of whom are talented in music composition. The pop musical circle shows the unprecedented colorfulness and prosperity. This new age is characterized as "masses' entertainment entertains the masses".

Cell-phone enables common people to have close contact with pop music. In 2001, more than 20 music radios together broadcast the program named "Chinese Song List", which introduces the original music to the audience nationwide for the first time. The program offers many activities such as "ordering songs by SMS" and "evaluating the songs", which give everyone the right to decide which song is good enough for "the golden song" and which singer can be honored as the best singer. It has been a common practice for programs of the

进入 21 世纪，国内外音乐资讯快速流通，人们的欣赏口味变得更加多样：R&B、韩流、朋克、流行+摇滚……歌坛新人辈出，而且大多具有优秀的创作能力。流行乐坛五彩缤纷，中国原创音乐空前活跃。"大众娱乐，娱乐大众"成为这一时期的特点。

手机的普及使人们开始与流行歌曲"零距离"接触。2001 年，20 家音乐电台联合推出"中国歌曲排行榜"节目，第一时间把原创音乐介绍给全国听众。排行榜开设短信点歌、点评，每个人都有权决定哪首歌是"金曲"、哪位歌手是"最佳"。媒体节目靠手机短信与听（观）众互动，成为惯例。

网络时代，不知有多少人的命运被网络改变。2004 年下半年诞生的网络歌曲

《老鼠爱大米》，到 2005 年 3 月，居然创造了一亿人次点击的纪录！普普通通的你，在网上上传一首自己演唱的歌曲，或许一夜之间就能"一曲成名"。2005 年，"我为歌狂"网络歌王争霸赛，让网络歌曲创作空前繁荣，网络歌曲进入了"工业化"时代，为中国流行乐坛注入了全新的活力。

"全民娱乐"精神在 2005 年湖南卫视的"超级女声"电视选秀活动中得到了超级体现。这个节目不仅让爱唱歌的女孩们圆了歌星梦，也让爱听歌的"粉丝"们有了投放热情的对象。2005 年超女冠军还登上了美国《时代》周刊的封面，被称为"平民英雄"。此外，"梦想中国"、"加油！好男儿"等节目个个火爆，"平民造星"运动席卷全国。

流行音乐，从遥不可及的舞台，真正走近了平凡人，我们的生活在音乐中变得精彩，不再平凡。

media to communicate with audiences by SMS.

Meanwhile, the newly appeared Internet changed many people's destinies. By the time of March, 2005, the popular song "Mouse Love Rice" on Internet has been hit over 100 million times. A common person can upload his own songs to the website, which may make him popular overnight. In 2005, the network singer contest "Crazy for Songs" brought unprecedented boom to the network songs which inject new energy to the circle of Chinese pop music.

The spirit "the people's music entertains the people" has been fully represented in the show of "Super Girls" on the channel of Hunan Satellite TV station in 2005. This program has not only fulfilled many girls' dream to be singing stars, but also provided the opportunities for music fans to exert their enthusiasm. The champion of "Super Girls" in 2005 even appeared on the cover of *Time* of the U.S. Similar programs such as "Chinese Dream", "Come on, Good Boy!" all become hits in recent years.

Pop music is now approaching common Chinese people from the once unreachable stage, which brings a lot of happiness and wonders to our life.